Exploring England's Heritage

DORSET TO GLOUCESTERSHIRE

Martin Robertson

Published in association with

English ⌗ Heritage

London: HMSO

Martin Robertson began working as Investigator of Historic Buildings for the Ministry of Housing and Local Government in 1968 (which was taken over by the Department of the Environment in 1971) and then transferred to English Heritage in 1986. He is now a Principal Inspector of Ancient Monuments and Historic Buildings, with special responsibility for historic buildings. The author lives both in a Grade 1 square in Bath and a Grade A house in Scotland, now carefully restored. He is especially interested in the history of transport and communications, is a Panel Member of the Railway Heritage Trust and an Associate of the Art Workers Guild. Martin Robertson is also a co-author of *The Railway Heritage of Britain*, and is currently writing a book about Bath.

Front cover: Stonehenge (detail) by John Constable. Courtesy of the Trustees of the V&A.

Back cover: Bristol Floating Harbour, looking east from Prince Street Bridge, with St Mary Redcliffe in the background. Martin Robertson

Frontispiece: Avebury, part of the stone circle. English Heritage

© Martin Robertson 1992
First published 1992
ISBN 0 11 300028 6

British Library Cataloguing in Publication Data
A CIP catalogue record for this book is available from the British Library

HMSO publications are available from:

HMSO Publications Centre
(Mail and telephone orders only)
PO Box 276, London, SW8 5DT
Telephone orders 071-873 9090
General enquiries 071-873 0011
(queuing system in operation for both numbers)

HMSO Bookshops
49 High Holborn, London, WC1V 6HB
071-873 0011 (counter service only)
258 Broad Street, Birmingham, B1 2HE
021-643 3740
Southey House, 33 Wine Street, Bristol, BS1 2BQ
0272-264306
9–21 Princess Street, Manchester, M60 8AS
061-834 7201
80 Chichester Street, Belfast, BT1 4JY
0232-238451
71 Lothian Road, Edinburgh, EH3 9AZ
031-228 4181

HMSO's Accredited Agents
(see Yellow Pages)

and through good booksellers

Printed in the UK for HMSO
Dd 293217   C80   3/92

Contents

Foreword

Today as midsummer approaches, Oxford is crammed with tourists. The roads near my office are choked with open-topped buses, their multilingual commentaries extolling the virtues of the city, while the pavements are impassable with crocodiles of visitors, eyes glued on the coloured umbrellas of determined guides. Dons wearing full academic dress attempt to make their way to and from the Examination Schools, to the delight of foreign photographers, and might as well be extras employed by the Tourist Board.

Oxford, Stratford-on-Avon and London together make up the golden triangle – golden, that is, to the tour operators – and millions of tourists are led through their crowded streets each year. The great majority of those who visit Oxford come for only a few hours, then move on to Stratford to stay overnight before returning to familiar London. It is London that takes the brunt. Westminster Abbey will be host to over 3 million, more than 2 million will visit the Tower of London, and then of course there are the museums and art galleries welcoming their annual tidal wave. Tourism, as governments are pleased to remind us, is one of Britain's biggest industries.

Looking at the tired, bewildered faces of the tourists off-loaded and scooped up again outside Oxford's St Giles, I long to grab them and say, 'It's all right – this is *not* what it's about. England is a beautiful, gentle country full of fascinating corners, breathtaking sights – an eclectic mix of insurpassable quality. All you need is someone with vision to show you how to start looking.'

Well, people with vision, as well as the knowledge of our cultural heritage and the ability to communicate, are not in ample supply, but the members of the team assembled to write the eleven volumes of *Exploring England's Heritage* share these qualities in abundance. Each author has a detailed and expert involvement, not only with the region they are writing about, but also with the buildings, the earthworks, the streets and the landscapes they have chosen to introduce us to. These guides are no mere compilations of well-worn facts, but original accounts coloured by the enthusiasm of people who know what makes a particular site so special.

Each volume introduces more than 100 places. Some are well known (who would dare to omit Stonehenge or Hadrian's Wall?); others are small-scale and obscure but no less interesting for that. We are led down alley-ways to admire hidden gems of architecture, into churchyards to search for inscribed stones and along canals to wonder at the skills of our early engineers. And of course there are the castles, the great houses and their gardens and the churches and cathedrals that give England its very particular character.

Exploring England's Heritage does not swamp you in facts. What each author does is to say, 'Let me show you something you might not have seen and tell you why I find it so particularly interesting.' What more could the discerning traveller want?

Barry Cunliffe

Acknowledgements

This book has arisen out of two things: my work and experience with the national resurvey of buildings of special architectural and historic interest, and my residence, since 1981, in the city of Bath. I should like to thank my stepfather Douglas Shepherdson for introducing me to the study of buildings; and my employers, first the Ministry of Housing and Local Government, then the Department of the Environment, and now English Heritage for giving me the experience. I wish to thank Brian Anthony for his editing, and my colleagues for their support and knowledge. British Rail (Intercity) provided me with workspace, but for this I had to pay. I have been helped with practical things by Stephen Johnson; while Pamela Corben, Sylvia Archer and Christine White have shared the unpleasant task of typing my manuscript, for my handwriting is not 'user friendly'. I have been given advice and information by Dai Morgan Evans, Francis Kelly, Keith Falconer, Julian Orbach, David Jacques and Harriet Jordan, and my thanks go to all of them. Any facility evident in the writing is largely due to my mother, Nancy Shepherdson, and my partner Anina Hutton, who between them left no word unturned. Any economies of accuracy, which I shall call imagination, are wholly my own responsibility.

Author and publisher are grateful to the following for permission to reproduce their photographs: Britain on View (British Tourist Authority/English Tourist Board); Patrick Brown; Cambridge University Committee for Aerial Photography, © Crown copyright; *Country Life*; English Heritage; Lockyer & Son; Ministry of Defence, © Crown copyright 1992/MOD reproduced with the permission of the Controller of HMSO; Oxford County Libraries; Royal Commission on the Historical Monuments of England; South Avon Mercury; the SS *Great Britain* Project; Syndication International Ltd; and The Picture Company Ltd.

We are also thankful to the following for permission to adapt site plans from their original versions (gazetteer-entry numbers are given in bold): **4** R Goodburn, National Trust guide to Chedworth Roman villa; **6** E M Clifford and E Comm, *Antiquity* XL (1966), p132; **15** RCHME, *An Inventory of Historical Monuments in the County of Dorset: Volume Three – Central Dorset, Part 2*, London: HMSO, 1970, opp. p 263; **16** Henry Willis, *Pillboxes*, London: Leo Cooper (originally published by Secker & Warburg), 1985; **79** Alice Mary Hadfield, *The Chartist Land Company*, Newton Abbot: David & Charles, 1970.

Notes for the Reader

Each site entry in *Exploring England's Heritage* is numbered and may be located easily on the end-map, but it is recommended especially for the more remote sites that the visitor make use of the relevant Ordnance Survey map in the Landranger series. The location details of the site entries include a six-figure National Grid reference, e.g., SX 888609. Ordnance Survey maps show the National Grid and the following 1:50,000 maps will be useful: 149, 150, 151, 162, 163, 172, 173, 181, 182, 183, 184, 192, 193, 194 and 195.

Readers should be aware that while the great majority of properties and sites referred to in this handbook are normally open to the public on a regular basis, others are open only on a limited basis. A few are not open at all, and may only be viewed from the public thoroughfare. In these circumstances readers are reminded to respect the owners' privacy. The *access codes* which appear at the end of each gazetteer entry are designed to indicate the level of public accessibility, and are explained below.

Abbreviations

A	Avon
BP	Before Present
BTA/ETB	Britain on View, British Tourist Authority/English Tourist Board
CL	*Country Life*
CUCAP	Cambridge University Committee for Aerial Photography
D	Dorset
EH	English Heritage
G	Gloucestershire
LT	Landmark Trust
MR	Martin Robertson
NT	National Trust
PB	Patrick Brown
RCHME	Royal Commission on the Historical Monuments of England
SIL	Syndication International Ltd
S	Somerset
W	Wiltshire

Access Codes

[A] site open for at least part of the year
[B] site open by appointment only
[C] site open by virtue of its use, e.g., a road, theatre, church or cinema
[D] site not open but may be seen from the public highway or footpath

Further Information

Further details on English Heritage, the Landmark Trust and the National Trust may be obtained from the following addresses:

English Heritage, PO Box 1BB, London W1A 1BB
Landmark Trust, 21 Dean's Yard, Westminster, London SW1
National Trust, PO Box 39, Bromley, Kent BR1 1NH

Introduction

Over the last 5,000 years or so the landscape of the five counties of Avon, Dorset, Gloucestershire, Somerset and Wiltshire has been slowly subjugated to man, with the speed of change constantly accelerating, particularly since 1750. This is what heritage is, the effect of man on his surroundings, and the relics he leaves behind him for the use and instruction of those who come after. The survival of 'heritage' is thus a highly selective process in which choice, necessity, natural decay, and politics interfere, and these work together with our interpretive abilities to build up our perception and understanding of what has been left to us.

The past is a country which is very difficult to relate to, for the consistent overlay of the works of new ages and cultures on those already present puzzles the onlooker, who desperately tries to tie things together to aid understanding, and instead brings confusion upon himself. The teaching of an understanding of the past as something of relevance to us today is thankfully now undertaken in schools much more than before, and projects teaching 'living' history are actively encouraged. History was looked upon as a procession might be, with things appearing, going past and vanishing again – yet in reality they don't vanish, but merely leave the stage and add themselves to the ever-growing pile of evidence available to us. We live with the past as if in a room with forever-changing wallpaper, with new design features constantly being added to the old, but with the original bones of the design never quite vanishing entirely, and always ready, with a little research, cleaning, and conservation to appear once again, like crop marks during a dry summer, revealing an ancient structure perhaps suspected, or maybe entirely new to knowledge.

The five counties have seen this process as much as any part of England, with the ebb and flow of peoples across the face of their bold landscape forms, the largely unchanging chalk downs, the river valleys, and the great forests which were felled long ago and now, at last, can begin to make a comeback. The broad band of limestone hills stretching across from south-west to north-east, carrying the high wolds and providing the fine building stones for which this area was renowned, have done so much to form the architectural character of the towns and villages famous for the consistent quality of their buildings, and their great potential for photography and tourism. Tourists, indeed, may be forgiven for thinking that Bath or Cotswold stone was the only building material used in the days before concrete blocks, for most of the highly visited towns are built of stone – Bath (A), Chipping Campden (G), Devizes (W), and Bradford-on-Avon (W) for instance – but there is also a great deal of brick: Weymouth (D) is a largely brick town, as are Gloucester (G), Cheltenham (G), Taunton (S), Swindon (W) and Bournemouth (D), the brick often covered with render to give it the appearance at least of the stone which was fashionable, but not available in sufficient quantity or quality in the area.

Even standing buildings can 'disappear' – as in the case of **St Lawrence, Bradford-on-Avon** (31, W) where the true nature of the building as a Saxon church lay hidden for centuries until finally recognised by an expert eye. What the visitor to Bradford sees today is what a Victorian restorer thought this Saxon church may have looked like in the 10th century, confused by later alterations which destroyed the evidence of its original appearance, so that this had either to be invented, or the later alterations left to give a rather mystifying effect.

Extensive alterations to historic structures offer problems of interpretation and restoration which are impossible to work out to everyone's satisfaction. **Blackfriars, Gloucester** (23, G) is a case in point. This was a monastic house sold at the Dissolution and

Churchyard of St Mary the Virgin, Painswick, Gloucestershire. PB

1

Blackfriars, Gloucester, interior of east end of church. EH

converted, more or less thoroughly: the church into a house, 'Bell's Place', and the claustral buildings into workshops. After centuries of misuse it finally came to the Ministry of Works and, over the last thirty years, the friary has slowly and painstakingly been picked out from the later accretions, with all but the medieval fabric disappearing bit by bit. Problems soon appeared, however, for the medieval fabric survived only in part and thus, as the 16th, 17th and 18th centuries were stripped away, they have had to be replaced by modern materials and structures to prevent the building from becoming a ruin. The church,

which became the house, had been truncated at each extremity, the walls had been filled with 16th-century and Georgian windows, whole sections of the original roof and south wall had gone completely. It is now a house on the outside and a church of a kind on the inside, with the south wall mostly glass, the crossing roof mostly steel, and a good deal of concrete holding together the remaining medieval parts. Conservation is a curious idea at its best, with a monument frozen at a particular moment in time, and then kept by endless repair in this permanent limbo. Gloucester's Blackfriars is a particularly

good example of some possible results.

Stonehenge (10, W) and **Avebury** (1, W), too, now declared World Heritage Sites, have enjoyed extremely varied careers as ancient monuments. Stonehenge had its final period of development in the 2nd millennium BC, and has been left to its own devices for most of the last 2,000 years. Natural decay and stone robbing has meant that the monument has changed little by little, but its isolation has really kept this to a minimum. It has been recognised as a national curiosity at least since Charles II's reign, but the State finally took a decision that decay should cease, not, however, at the date when the decision was taken, but on an arbitrarily selected date in the 18th century. The monument was reconstructed in 1957 to match its appearance in the late 18th century, thus rendering invalid its most memorable images, the paintings of Turner and Constable.

As a child in the 1950s I was brought up in the processional theory of history in which you worked through the past from the Romans on in a hopeless endeavour to catch up with yourself. Prehistory was a world completely apart from reality, presumably because there were no written records. Monuments such as Stonehenge were prehistoric for the simple reason that if they had been built any later someone would have recorded it. This idea is a fallacy, anyway, since almost nothing was recorded as other than the arena for a political event until the antiquaries of the late 16th and 17th centuries took a hand, while prehistoric origins can now often be proved scientifically. My hazy ideas about the age of Stonehenge were rudely shattered on visiting the site for the first time in 1957, and finding, as luck would have it, one of the stones actually hanging in mid-air! Theories of age and method of construction were blown away; I had seen it done, and ever since have known exactly how old Stonehenge is.

My scepticism concerning the authenticity of ancient monuments has survived the years, and indeed has been strengthened if anything by experience. I remember in the 1950s seeing a medieval wall being built at the Bishops Palace at St David's, Dyfed. The 1980s have seen a harbour appear at Threave Castle in Scotland, not to be found on the colour postcards available at the site. The Avebury you visit today only dates from 1939 when Alexander Keiller had finished reconstructing it from the stones found broken and buried on the site, for many of them had been deliberately buried in the Middle Ages, while others were smashed in the 18th century, as William Stukeley recorded. The site is much more instructive as a result, but how many of today's visitors realise that the stones have not been standing 'time

out of mind' as I had so innocently believed at Stonehenge?

Almost every site in this book should be viewed with some suspicion, for it is not necessarily what it seems. Most of the antiquities have been edited in some way. All displayed long barrows for instance have been rebuilt to some degree, while the chalk-cut hill figures have been altered, or even changed completely. The latter provide another example of how little, in the past, the English have shown any curiosity about even the most obvious of antiquities. The **Cerne Giant** (3, D) is outstandingly obvious and yet there is no record of it until 1742. It appears to be ancient, but

does it really date from shortly before that time? If it had been newish then surely they would have said so? The Roman sites too were very abused by the Victorian diggers, who left them in a condition suited to their own interpretations, and then often made sure there was no written record to confuse the issue.

Fortifications have posed other problems. The Iron Age hillforts used to be thought of as coming to a sudden end in terms of development and use after the Roman invasion, but the full explorations of **Maiden Castle** (17, D) and **Cadbury Castle** (13, S) have shown that they continued in use long after

Raising the capstone of a trilithon at Stonehenge. EH

3

House built from broken sarsens at Avebury. MR

that. The present condition of stone castles was largely imagined to have been the result of the Civil War, 'ruins that Cromwell knocked about a bit'. Some he did, but many were already in ruins, while others suffered major collapses only many years later, like at **Nunney** (18, S) in 1910. Often subjective editing has coloured our view of what remains. We see Nunney as a sort of jewel-like tower house standing within a moat, just as we do Tattershall in Lincolnshire, but both once had extensive circuit walls, demolished for the convenience of owners, and must have then looked very different from their present appearance.

With monuments out of use it is much easier to pinpoint the moment when decay was halted and 'preservation' began. This may often be the day when a monument was handed over to the keeping of the State or the National Trust; but there may also have been a decision to return it to its supposed condition at an arbitrarily selected moment in the past, as happened with Stonehenge, or to a condition it never enjoyed, as at Avebury where they simply re-erected all the stones they could find (though the fate of some at least is plain enough, for the broken remains can be seen built into the houses in Avebury village still standing within the circle).

Churches are a thorny case, for buildings in use for ecclesiastical purposes are still outside the planning controls effective on other buildings, and the churches themselves have determined the way in which they have grown and changed over the centuries. Thus there are examples of unaltered churches from every period, as there are ones which have been changed materially as often as possible. The gazetteer illustrates both kinds and shows how many types of alteration there might be. Large country houses have developed organically, just as churches do, but listed building controls have meant that an arbitrary stop has been placed on this growth, so that any further developments are not only brought about through the requirements of the users but are also subject to the opinions that planning and national advisory bodies may have about a house's importance as a part of the national built heritage.

Parks and gardens are even more subject to natural change and decay than buildings, and over a much shorter time-scale. They have been subjected to fashion, economy, drought and abandonment as well as the changes wrought by the introduction of new plants and materials. They can disappear entirely under new designs, and reappear again if any historically minded owner decides to recreate what was there before. **Westbury Court** (70, G) is an almost exact recreation of the garden's appearance in 1712. It seems never to have been extensively redesigned during its life, fell into complete decay and is now new again. **Stourhead** (69, W) has always been maintained to its finally developed design of the late 18th century, but its character was greatly changed by extensive planting of the newly available flowering shrubs in the 19th century, and these are now partly being removed again. **Hestercombe** (66, S) too, though a garden of this century, is being completely restored to its original design from a state of dereliction, while the closely contemporary **Hidcote** (67, G) has developed over the years, and has always been maintained to the highest standards. There are also two kinds of public park: the municipal amenity park incorporating playgrounds and tennis courts in the design, and the educational ones, represented here by a botanic garden and an arboretum. An attempt has been made to cover the range of landscape history, as well as the differing garden types so well represented in this particular region.

This guide explores the riches of the area's vernacular architecture in its group context within the towns and villages. Beyond this, such houses can really only be understood by visiting a number of examples, and in particular noting the interior planning and the construction. This is outside the scope of a guide designed to promote visits by the public, for small houses are not

Bradford-on-Avon town and bridge. MR

generally open, or even available to be looked at closely except in the village context. A certain amount can be learnt from the outside of such houses, but the information is often very misleading and can only be sorted out with a full inspection, and that is not going to be available to the average visitor. Some house types are mentioned, for instance the wool merchants' and clothiers' houses of which many splendid examples exist in Bradford-in-Avon, Devizes, Trowbridge (W), Painswick (G), and **Chipping Campden** (41, G) among others, but the range is too great for one to attempt a proper coverage here.

There is, however, one type of housing which is particularly well represented in the five counties and that is the planned village. The examples of these are interesting both for their design, and for the background from which they sprang. Some have an agricultural background, having been built as model villages to improve the conditions of estate workers (**Grittleton**, 75, W) or to remove their older habitations from too close a proximity with the landowner (**Milton Abbas**, 76, D). Others were built as experiments, like the Chartist Land Settlement at **Snig's End** (79, G), something that was intended to be the beginnings of a major shift in landownership, but doomed to failure once the landed establishment realised that it threatened their own positions. Then there are the industrial housing schemes (naturally much more common in the north), of which the **Swindon Railway Village** (80, W) is a particularly thoroughgoing example, due to the farsightedness of the Great Western Railway, and, of course to its designer, Brunel, who saw it as a part of

an integrated work settlement of the highest efficiency. Finally **Tolpuddle** (82, D) is a memorial not to architecture at all, but to all workers who have suffered injustice at their employer's hands.

This leads on to the second group of buildings, those connected with education, entertainment and the law: college, theatre, inn, workhouse, law court and prison, all famous examples even in the national context, and characteristic of their building types as well as giving insights into the society from which they sprang. Eighteenth- and 19th-century reformers, such as John Howard, Dr Thomas Arnold and Charles Dickens, brought about changes in society as significant as those wrought by the Industrial Revolution, leading to educational, social and municipal improvements of all kinds and the laying down of the infrastructure still largely in use today. During the 20th century, agriculture has changed enormously, so that the majority of traditional buildings and farming practices are redundant, and much of the actual appearance of the farmland has changed completely.

Today's transport system, however, is still largely that of the Victorians. The railways are more intensively used over a much reduced system. The roads, apart from the relatively few motorways, are still basically the turnpike roads as taken over by the government in the 1880s. Widened, realigned, and covered in tarmac they may be, but the ancient and Roman roads, the roads described by John Ogilby in 1675, the 18th-century turnpikes, are all still represented in the national system. In just the same way, bridges from all periods continue in all

levels of use. It would be interesting to know the earliest bridge still in use on a trunk road, but there are certainly a number of medieval ones carrying loads far in excess of anything their original builders may have contemplated.

What then is the message left us by the heritage of these five counties? The message which makes their heritage worth exploring, and of value to us today. In England, perhaps as much as anywhere, we are inextricably involved in our own past, surrounded on every side by the sites and relics it has left us, if we can read them. Everyone is a tourist in this, whether they are visiting someone else's past, or their own, and guides are needed to aid appreciation and understanding. The sites described here are only a scratching of the surface, chosen to represent different types and give enjoyable visits. They are not necessarily the best or most complete examples, but are personal favourites and, as such, will not necessarily be the personal favourites of others. If someone is encouraged to look where they have not looked before, and find examples they think better, then the book has done a job worth doing. The past can be enjoyed everywhere, for everywhere man's hand is on the face of the land, and that, in whatever aspect, is what heritage is. It is curious to think that we live in the midst of other countries and other cultures, one laid on another, each editing the remains of those that have gone before. It is a world of surprises where nothing can be taken at face value. When you have seen the stones of Stonehenge hanging from a crane the message comes over more clearly. Tread carefully, and look well, for in the past nothing is what it seems.

Antiquities: Prehistoric, Roman and Post-Roman

These five counties are particularly rich in antiquities, especially field monuments of the prehistoric period when, according to all surviving evidence, this area had a large, well-organised population capable of major endeavour. **Stonehenge** (10, W), **Silbury Hill** (8, W) and **Maiden Castle** (17, D) demonstrate that England before the Romans, however shadowy in terms of history, was inhabited by a series of peoples with social arrangements, technology and determination on levels which can be compared with other ancient civilisations which, through their more glamorous remains, have attracted public attention. The progress of people, from the Neolithic period down through the Bronze and Iron Ages until the Roman invaders brought the British cultures to an abrupt subjugation in the 1st century AD, is marked upon our landscape.

With the improvements in scientific methods of archaeology, and with air photography, we now have much more information about the scale of settlement, the details of agriculture, and society at the various periods. Constantly expanding data has led to a continued reassessment of evidence. Interpretation is not easy since we are very much the prisoners of our own level of knowledge. Our study of ancient cultures is dependent not just on what has survived, which of course tends to be the least destructible of artefacts, and which may in itself give an unbalanced picture, but also on what we have so far found, and the meaning we attach to it. To the 17th-century antiquaries the great henges, the banks and ditches, the long and round barrows and the hundreds of hillforts appeared to be all more or less of the same age, simply pre-Roman, and other post-Roman remains such as **Wansdyke** (22, W, A) would have been confused with them, giving a quite erroneous idea of prehistoric society. Close studies of

Stonehenge and **Avebury** (1, W) made in more recent times, have shown that, like the great hillforts, they were developed over a considerable period and were not necessarily the work of one people.

It would be natural to assume that the long barrows and chambered tombs are a development from the simpler round barrows, but they actually belong to the Stone Age, before the arrival of metal tools. As with Silbury Hill and the henges, excavation and close study have revealed the full complexity of their construction – with the earth carefully stabilised within by dry-stone walls and standing megaliths (orthostats) – and this, together with their much greater size, has enabled these fine mounds to survive the centuries, and the plough, more successfully than the smaller and younger round barrows. Any visitor without this background knowledge might imagine that these two forms of barrow are of the same period, producing an idea of a more stratified society with some people meriting large barrows, and some small ones. Although this is clearly not the case, very little is really known about who merited burial in this way, but we must assume from the effort involved and from the quality of the artefacts found within them that they were only for the elite. There are particularly good collections of artefacts from the barrows in the Wiltshire County Museum at Salisbury and the Dorset County Museum in Dorchester.

The barrows described here are chosen to represent both periods. **Hetty Pegler's Tump** (6, G) is a fine chambered tomb (not all long barrows have this complex construction) of what is called the Severn-Cotswold group which comprise the country's largest and finest group of such monuments. The Bronze Age round barrows at **Badbury Rings** (2, D) are less interesting to visit since they cannot be entered, but are seen as contributions to the landscape and the sense of the past and

Roman mosaic pavement from Barton Farm, Cirencester, now in Corinium Museum. Drawing by John Beecham.
RCHME

have been chosen for their particularly impressive siting.

After the Roman conquest of 43–44 AD Wessex became one of the earliest and most comprehensively settled areas of Roman occupation, and Roman influence seems to have lasted longer than in other parts. Rome withdrew the legions and largely abandoned the province in 410, but the area remained Romano-British due to the Arthurian-inspired rearguard winning a famous victory against English invaders at Mons Badonicus in about 500. The English were not finally successful in the area until the Battle of Dyrham gave them control in 577. With Rome in control of the area for a period of several hundred years, it would be surprising if the survival of remains of all kinds were not very common, but it must be remembered that what have survived are, in the main, the more solidly built structures of the wealthy, the military and the civil administration.

The collapse of the Roman way of life in Britain, and the redundancy of their towns and villas for a period of centuries, has meant that standing monuments have survived only when either very substantial, or very isolated, such as the wilder parts of Hadrian's wall; town and fort walls could later be reused, such as those at Colchester in Essex where the Roman gate still survives in use, or at Porchester Castle in Hampshire, one of the forts of the Saxon shore. The wilfulness of history has meant, however, that some extremely fine and delicate artefacts have survived and there are many very beautiful mosaic pavements still almost complete – the 'Orpheus' pavement in the churchyard at Woodchester (G) is the most elaborate, but several very fine ones can be seen in the Corinium Museum. Corinium (Cirencester, G) was Roman Britain's second city, and at Aquae Sulis (Bath) there survives probably the finest Roman civil monument in the country, the **Roman Baths** (7, A) themselves. A number of good villas have survived, of which that at **Chedworth** (4, G) has been selected. Witcombe (G) is also displayed fully and King's Weston in Bristol (A) is laid out. There must be many more which are

still unknown in this very rich agricultural area.

Some good examples of Roman fortifications and roads are discussed in chapters 2 and 9. Another category of antiquity, chalk-cut hill figures, occur more commonly in this region than in any other part of the country. Their provenance is again mysterious for if they are genuinely ancient, as some appear to be, it is strange that there is no record of them earlier than the 18th century. They are both obvious and remarkable so why did nobody think it worth while describing or even mentioning them? The English seem to have become curious about their own past only fairly recently, and presumably accepted all ancient things as being semi-natural and largely beyond understanding. It took John Aubrey's interest in Wiltshire to provoke wider recognition of Stonehenge and Avebury; he visited the area with Charles II and James, Duke of York, in 1665. Inigo Jones had described Stonehenge (quite inaccurately) in 1655, but before that educated people saw interest only in Greece and Rome. Interest in British antiquities was probably actively discouraged by the Church because of their pagan origins and popular association with magic. They remain, however, our chief passport to the distant past and an interest in and understanding of them is crucial to the understanding of the continuity of our history, a continuity still to be seen in all its phases in the much used and abused English landscape.

1

Avebury, Wiltshire
Neolithic, c.2500 BC

SU 102699. In Avebury village, 7 miles W of Marlborough

[A] EH NT

The A4361 as it crosses the Avebury henge monument must run in the oldest course of all, for it still uses the causewayed entrances built some 4,500 years ago. It is one of the few Neolithic sites still in use today, although hardly for its original purpose, whatever that

may have been. Samuel Pepys visited on his summer tour in 1668 and saw 'a place trenched in like Old Sarum almost with great stones pitched in it some bigger than those at Stonage [*sic*] in figure to my great admiration'. His comparison with Old Sarum is very exact as far as size is concerned, for the ramparts of both surround some thirty acres. But Avebury apparently had no defensive purpose, the ditch being inside the rampart and thus a hindrance to defenders, and it is a considerable ditch, being originally 30 ft deep and flat-bottomed. This must be a ritual enclosure constructed with enormous effort, and demonstrating the qualities of determination and organisation inherent in the society of the day: those qualities which are even more dramatically displayed at nearby, roughly contemporary Silbury (8, W).

The surviving monument is in two parts: the three small circles within, which are the first build, and the great circle with its attendant earthworks, which are the later redesign. This is fairly complete in the western quadrants, with the stones largely gone from the eastern. One does not have to look far to see where. The sarsens or 'grey wethers' were taken, smashed and built into the village houses where they remain to this day. William Stukeley recorded this happening in the 1720s, so Pepys would have seen more stones in place than we do now. Curiously enough, however, the ones he saw are mostly those that were smashed, while the ones we see today are mainly those buried on the Church's orders in the Middle Ages and found and re-erected by Alexander Keiller in the 1930s. Our monument has only existed since 1939 and at no other period in its history.

Though similar to Stonehenge (10, W) in design, date and presumably use, Avebury is in many ways different. Larger and yet more intimate, busy with traffic and yet much quieter with people. Go to the east gate, climb the rampart and look out to the east and the south, and you come as near to Neolithic England as you can realistically get.

Reconstruction drawing of Avebury, by Alan Sorrell. EH

Badbury Rings hillfort from the air. RCHME. Inset: round barrows and Roman Road. MR

2

Barrows at Badbury Rings, Dorset
Bronze Age c. 2000–500 BC

ST 960030. On B3082 4 miles NW of Wimborne Minster

[A] NT

Bronze Age round barrows are not merely 'humps and bumps' as they are so unkindly known by the non-archaeologist, but have significant landscape qualities, particularly on the chalk downlands of Wessex where so many can be seen, adding their presence to the often magical emptiness and the song of the skylark. What are they other than mounds of earth heaped over long-stolen corpses from a far-off age? Today's archaeologist with modern scientific methods finds them much more than that, for they cover and protect the land surface of 3,000 years ago with its seeds, insects and pollen, which can tell us much about life in the distant past. Probably all barrows have been robbed, many in the 18th century, often using the most primitive methods, and with only the most outstanding finds kept or recorded, giving an unbalanced view of the high quality of the Wessex culture.

It is probable that the barrows were built only for the quality folk and their possessions, for there was a lot of work in them, but we must not impose our own hierarchical ideas upon a culture of which little is really known. Homer speaks of raising mounds in a day to honour the dead, but the Greeks made much use of slaves, and maybe the Wessex folk did as well. There are thousands of round barrows of various types (bowl, ring, disc, etc.) in Wessex. Many can be seen from Stonehenge (10, W), in the Avebury area (1, W), and there is a fine group where the Ridgeway (103, W) meets the A4, but the ones featured are a particularly dramatic group in eastern Dorset. They are the six situated along the finely preserved stretch of Roman road which skirts Badbury Rings near Wimborne. This is again a magnificent hillfort with a double circuit of ramparts of great size, and the three monuments together, the barrows, the road and the fort make a combined visit of great interest.

3

Cerne Giant, Dorset
Romano-British, 200–500 AD

ST 666017. E of A352, about 1 mile N of Cerne Abbas

[A] NT

Much loved by small children of all ages, the Cerne Giant is an arresting sight, and the inhabitants of the ancient village of Cerne Abbas have never quite known whether or not to point to it with pride. If it is truly Romano-British – and this seems likely since it is hard to imagine when else it might date from – then its survival is the result of careful tending down the centuries, with the blessing of

Cerne Giant. BTA/ETB

the monks through the medieval period and the local church since. The earliest record of its existence is 1742. Such chalk-cut figures need constant attention – usually an annual scouring which came to be a local holiday with attendant fair and excitement – and without this the encroaching turf would bring about a complete disappearance within a very few years. The modern applications of concrete, paint, weedkiller etc., though effective, are a good deal less romantic.

What does the figure represent? He is commonly thought to be a Romano-British Hercules, a cult figure symbolic of strength and fertility who enjoyed a revival in the reign of Commodus in the 1st century. Though 182 ft long, he is not quite the tallest man in England, as this honour goes to the very elongated and even more mysterious Wilmington Long Man in Sussex, but he is far more completely represented. Studies of the Uffington White Horse in Oxfordshire have demonstrated the change in form and character of such a monument through the centuries, so it is difficult to know if the Cerne Giant now represents his ancient appearance or whether he is the product of more skilful (and ruder) designers in the 17th or 18th century. It is known that he had a navel in the 18th century. The many legends concerning the Giant's possible magic properties, particularly those concerning young women hopeful of childbearing, are understandable. The cutting of such figures on the chalk downs of England became a common occurrence in later times, horses being the usual form (Westbury White Horse, 11, W). The provenance of some is clear but others, like the Cerne Giant, remain shrouded in mystery, if nothing else.

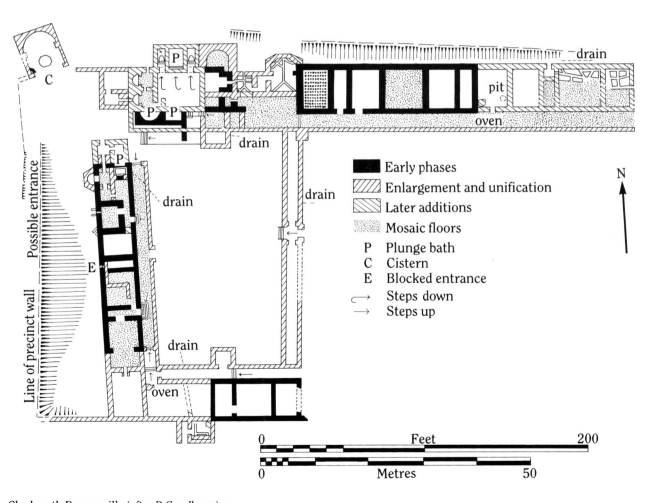

Chedworth Roman villa (after R Goodburn). EH

4

Chedworth Roman Villa, Gloucestershire
Mid-2nd century onwards

SP 070117. 7 miles N of Cirencester, between A435 and A429

[A] NT

The Chedworth villa poses many problems of interpretation not least because the first excavation, carried out with savagery and despatch by James Farrer in 1864, destroyed much of what evidence there was and left, as the only written record, a lecture given to the Society of Antiquaries of Scotland. The museum contains a larger selection of dressed stone than any other villa site, but we know neither where these specimens were found, nor how much of the 19th-century surviving whole they represent. It is a curious place to have chosen for settlement, high (500 ft above sea level) and cold, being shaded in winter, but great care was obviously taken with its siting, for it stands on an elaborately engineered platform, and the buildings were exceptionally well

Hypocaust at Chedworth Roman villa. MR

appointed. It has a spring, which is a rarity on the high Cotswold plateau, and this is probably the key to the choice of situation.

This villa, like most others, is the product of a series of building periods (six have been identified), which linked primarily free-standing buildings into a unified whole, giving what is commonly understood to be the appearance of a Roman villa. Large ranges of both dry- and wet-heated baths were built here and extended in several places – an unusual feature which might be accounted for by the cold climate. Uses other than that of a villa (the house of an agricultural estate) have been suggested, including some of ritual or religious significance, to account for the slightly odd position and planning of the building. Luckily it is now evident that the Victorian excavation did not unearth everything. A more scholarly investigation by Sir Ian Richmond in 1958–65 and by others again in 1977 and 1978 have shown that the south wing extends much further than was realised. This has not been excavated and may yet reveal new information.

5

Cirencester Roman Town, Gloucestershire
1st century–6th century AD

SP 024016. Cirencester town centre
[A] EH

Despite fifteen years of scientific excavation during the 1960s and 1970s, perhaps only 5 per cent of the area of Cirencester Roman Town (Corinium) has been dug. It was the second town of Roman Britain in size, exceeded only by London (Londinium). The town's importance lay in its being the civil capital in the centre of the early Roman frontier which was set roughly along the Cotswold escarpment following the Claudian invasion of 43 AD. Legionary fortresses were set up at Lincoln (Lindum) and Exeter (Isca Dumnorum) and the Fosseway (98) was built between them, linking the early towns of Cirencester and Bath (Aquae Sulis) on the way.

The Roman method of colonisation was to build a new capital near an existing tribal capital and then force the native population to move into their area of control (as was the case at Maiden Castle, 17, D). Corinium Dobunnorum replaced the tribal capital of the Dobunni at Bagendon Camp some 4 km to the north. The town expanded rapidly and by the end of the 1st century the road pattern (now sadly obliterated) had been established and public buildings erected. The military fortress, which has been partly excavated, was built by 90 AD. Complicated mural defences, together with monumental gates, have been found, as well as the forum and the amphitheatre, a theatre, houses and shops. The forum has unfortunately been entirely built over, but the amphitheatre is an extensive relic, demonstrating the large local population. No temples have been found, though they must have existed. There are few extra-mural buildings, and little sign of agricultural activity in the immediate vicinity, though extensive quarrying took place, as did the production of tiles, bricks and mosaics. A number of high-quality pavements using unusual mixtures of natural stones with glazed and unglazed tiles are shown in the museum.

The town appears to have remained important well into the 6th century, as it is mentioned in the *Anglo-Saxon Chronicle* in relation to the Battle of Dyrham in 577 when the Saxon invaders at last overcame the Arthurian-inspired Romano-British resistance.

6

Hetty Pegler's Tump or Uley Tumulus, Gloucestershire
Neolithic, 2500 BC

SO 790000. On W side of B4066 Stroud–Dursley road
[A] EH

Hetty Pegler's Tump is one of the best surviving examples of the long barrows known as the 'Severn-Cotswold' group. These barrows share characteristics of design and construction which may indicate a reasonably common origin.

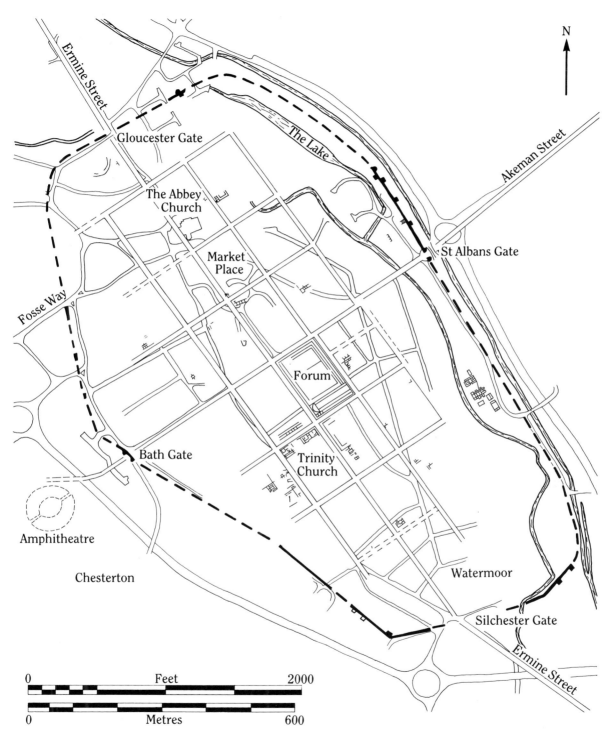

Cirencester Roman town. Corinium Dubunnorum. EH

They are mounds of great size, and were constructed using an elaborate system of dry-stone walling and standing monoliths or 'orthostats' to stabilise the soil and outline the internal passages and burial chambers. This construction can be most readily seen at nearby Nympsfield Barrow (1 mile north-west of Nympsfield on the B4066), which lacks its earth covering. The barrows are in two groups, those with true entrances as at Uley and Nympsfield, and others with false entrances to distract grave robbers as at Belas Knap (2 miles south of Winchcombe near Charlton Abbots) where the interior can also be visited.

Hetty Pegler's Tump (named after a landowner in the 17th century) is 120 ft long and 10 ft high. The interior has a central passageway leading to an end chamber, and two side chambers on the left or south side. The north passage wall is a conjectural reconstruction but is known to have fronted two matching northern chambers, one of which was destroyed in 1821 by workmen seeking stone. At that time the barrow was described by J T Lloyd-Baker as being in a fairly disturbed state. The barrow today is largely the result of the excavation and reconstruction undertaken by Dr John Thurnham in 1854, and subsequent repairs in 1872, 1891 and 1906. Uley was one of the original fifty monuments scheduled under the 1882 Act, but over the years its treatment has shown a cavalier disregard for authenticity and the value of recording. The result is, however, still satisfactory to visitors and is as damp and spooky as any child could require. Little is known about the builders of these oldest monuments, but the work involved shows these barrows must have been of great importance to them.

7

Roman Baths, Bath, Avon
1st–4th century

ST 751647. Bath town centre

[A]

The Roman Baths are generally agreed to be the single most impressive non-military survival from Roman Britain. The site is also of interest for the overlying medieval and Tudor baths, and the Georgian Pump Room above, but

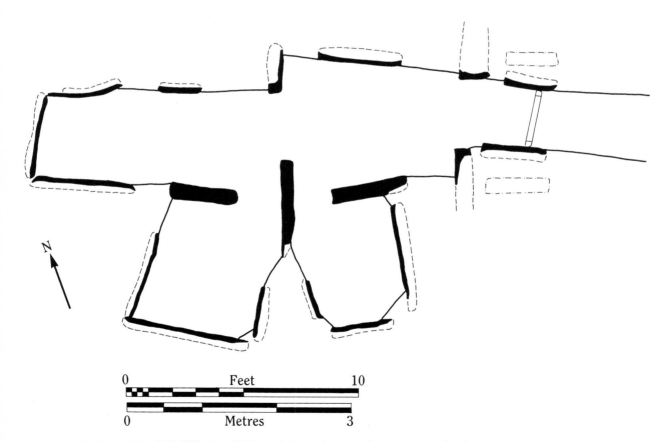

Hetty Pegler's Tump (after E M Clifford and E Camm). Dotted areas indicate re-erected orthostats. EH

The Great Bath looking east, with Bath Abbey. RCHME

here we concentrate on the Roman remains. The hot springs, whichever apocryphal source you follow, were clearly known before the Romans arrived and both their mystic and their healing properties were of interest to the invaders. It was the Romans' habit to incorporate local beliefs into their own already bewildering array, and everyone knows how keen they were on washing. The site was known to be a Roman one in the 18th century, the surviving Lucas bath being discovered in the 1760s – but it was not until the discovery of the 1st-century Great Bath by the City Architect Major C E Davis in 1878 that their true splendour and significance became apparent. The Great Bath (83 ft by 40 ft) stood in a hall measuring 110 ft by 68 ft with a brick-vaulted roof. The bath retains its lead lining and original inlet and outlet pipes, and is magnificent indeed, although the colour of the water is less than tempting.

The present, rather misleading, arrangement of colonnades and sculpture-lined parapets is Major Davis's attractive whimsy and dates from 1878–80. Since Barry Cunliffe's further excavations of 1971–2 and 1979–82, far more of the baths are displayed, in a very

imaginative and (in engineering terms) quite astonishing way. How many visitors think of the heavy splendours of the Pump Room above them? The full range of Roman water treatments survives with dates varying over a 300-year period. Finally there is the hot spring itself, now easier to see but no longer as romantic as it was before it was opened up. The water flows out from the Roman culvert, at a rate of half a million gallons a day, at a constant temperature of 47°C. As it gradually cools it is used in the different baths and is finally carried off to the Avon by the original Roman drain.

8

Silbury Hill, Wiltshire
c. 2700 BC

SU 100680. S of Avebury and on N side of A4 between West Kennet and Beckhampton

[D] EH

Despite several detailed investigations Silbury Hill remains as mysterious as ever: it does not appear to be a burial mound and we do not know what other

purpose it might have had. Shafts dug both from the summit and the sides have shown the full complexity of the construction of the mound, and computations about the amount of labour involved have been made. It is the largest artificial mound in Europe, covering 5½ acres, and it stands about 130 ft high. The construction was a very careful one using chalk blocks to build huge steps which were later filled in with the local river silt to produce the present rounded outline. This has proved to be a very strong construction and the soil has moved little since, though the ditch, once 20 ft deep and 70 ft wide, has silted up. The immense amount of material required was obtained from the ditch, from the original hill slope which ran through the base of the monument, and from local quarrying. The construction is such that it has been designated a Historic Engineering Work by the Institution of Civil Engineers, the oldest such monument in their register.

The investigations of the mound are of interest in themselves. The Duke of Northumberland brought Cornish miners to sink a shaft from the top in 1777, a period of extremely basic archaeological technique. They found nothing, and may have ensured that nobody else did either. In subsequent attempts several tunnels were dug into the sides in the 19th century but these were also unsuccessful. Details of construction were recorded by Professor Richard Atkinson in 1968–70, and these show it to have been built in three stages, but over a relatively short period of time. The dating can be made fairly accurately from the plant and insect remains on the original land surface and in the first added soil. It has been calculated that, with the technology of the time, some 7,000 man-years were needed to build Silbury Hill, an extraordinary figure which indicates the size of the local population and the importance of this mound to them. The Romans appear to have used it as a sighting point for laying out the Bath road, which skirts it on the south side, while the Saxons may have had a look-out post on the top.

With its surrounding ditch filled with

water, as happens occasionally in the winter, it looks just like a giant's sandcastle. It would be a pity to know everything about the past, and Silbury Hill continues to hold its secrets.

9

Stanton Drew Stone Circles, Avon
c.*500 BC*

ST 601629. 11 miles W of Bath, S of B3130 and close to village of Stanton Drew. Behind Manor House and St Mary's Vicarage

[A] EH

The remarkable quality of Stanton Drew is that so many of the stones survive in their original positions, a far higher proportion than is the case at Stonehenge or Avebury. Despite being the third largest collection of standing stones in England it is a very low-key monument; it still retains its Ministry of Works cast-iron plates and the complete dearth of information so familiar from monument visiting in the past. One reason for this, of course, is that nobody knows the significance of these circles or the use to which they were put. It is always imagined that they were intended for religious rituals, but they may have been concerned with the passing of the seasons, for some magical purpose, or to protect people in times of stress or when the sky threatened to fall. Certainly such stones continue to have a fascination, and they always have a calming effect on children, who are interested in their inexplicable nature, the work involved in erecting them and in the feel of the stones themselves.

These stones are very different from the sarsens of Salisbury Plain for they are the local lias with very uneven colour and texture and full of interesting holes. There are three circles in all: 370 ft, 97 ft and 130 ft in diameter. The largest is certainly the most impressive,

Silbury Hill under construction, showing the stepped form and the drystone walling. Realisation by Judith Dobie. EH

consisting of twenty-four stones with apparently only two missing. It has a short avenue as does the second circle. The cove nearby is a group of four stones which appears to be the chamber of a barrow, but the earth has long gone. There is also a solitary stone at Hautville's Quoit, about ½ mile away, which seems to have a geographic relationship to the circles. There is some indication of a ditch on one side but this may only be the remains of a hollow trackway. Although Stanton Drew lacks the majesty of the better known circles and has a less impressive setting, it can be enjoyed in timeless tranquillity in a way that Stonehenge and Avebury can never be.

10

Stonehenge, Wiltshire
Neolithic, Bronze and Iron Age, 2500–c.800 BC

SV 123422. On A344 by junction with A303, 2 miles W of Amesbury

[A] EH

This is the premier megalithic monument of Europe and easily the most visited of all British prehistoric sites. The site evolved over a very long period to reach its final and most elaborate form, and then, on abandonment in the Roman period, fell into gradual decay and dismemberment.

Stanton Drew, one of three circles. EH

Stonehenge, the central group of sarsens with some of the bluestones. EH

11
Westbury White Horse, Wiltshire
1778

ST 898516. S of the B3098 between Bratton and Westbury

[A] EH

The Westbury White Horse, one of a number which grace the chalk downs of Wessex, is known to date in its present form from the late 18th century. It is a strange creature, being upright and rather boxy in shape with elongated extremities, and one large round eye. It is much more stylised than either of the horses at Pewsey or Weymouth, which are probably also 18th century. The present Westbury figure is known to have replaced a more ancient-looking horse, like the one at Uffington in Oxfordshire, which faced in the opposite direction. This earlier horse was traditionally associated with the victory of the West Saxons under King Alfred at Ethandun in 878, a victory which forced the retreat of the invading Danes back to eastern England, and led to a period of peace and prosperity for Wessex. The battle ranged to the south of the escarpment, but the last stand and ultimate defeat of the Danes was probably among the ramparts of Bratton Castle; the white horse is on those ramparts, and is supposed to have been first cut by the victorious Saxons.

The Westbury horse, with the Cerne Giant (3, D) is the most striking of the Wessex hillside figures, being visible for a considerable distance, and was long kept clean by an annual scouring fair in June. The surface has now been concreted for easy maintenance. It, and the castle ramparts above, provide problems in conservation through their over-use by the public, with footpaths and motorcycles damaging the outlines. The castle, which dates from the Iron Age, is a bivallate promontory fort (a headland on the escarpment which has been surrounded by twin ditches and ramparts). There is also a round barrow and a long barrow on the site.

Westbury White Horse. BTA/ETB

The isolation of the site has to some extent protected the stones from removal and reuse, and their strange magical quality must have helped, but their very paganism led to deliberate destruction at the instigation of the Church. Damage in this way happened to a much greater extent at Avebury (1, W). The stones have also fallen naturally in the course of time but the present state of the monument is that of the 18th century, Professor Richard Atkinson having re-erected only one trilithon and a number of the other stones in 1957 to match its condition at that time.

It is necessary to consult the guidebook for the full details of the different phases of construction and the monument's subsequent history. In its final phase, the remains of which we see today, it consisted of a bank and ditch forming a circle about 110 m in diameter. An entrance on the north-east connects this with the Avenue within the banks of which the Hele Stone still stands. At the centre of the enclosure there stands the remains of a dressed sarsen stone peristyle about 30 m in diameter and nearly 5 m high, and within this is the blue stone circle.

Inside the circle there is most of a horseshoe setting of sarsen trilithons, the largest of the five being 7 m high. Inside this again is a blue stone horseshoe. Near to the centre is the recumbent stone called the altar stone.

The seemingly miraculous carriage of the blue stones from West Wales, and of the transport and erection of the sarsens which, though admittedly local, are of enormous size, continues to fascinate visitors, as do the more difficult questions concerning its purpose, its possible use as an observatory, as a Druidic temple, or any connection it may have with ley lines and other aspects of mysticism. A connection with the summer and winter solstices seems certain.

Despite the crude surroundings and the vast numbers of visitors, Stonehenge in its landscape rises above it all. The monument is currently undergoing a complete reassessment of its setting and presentation, which can only improve on the present inadequate display. If you find it too small then you must go to Avebury. If you look upon Stonehenge as a sophisticated construction of the earliest people, you cannot help but wonder at it.

Castles and Fortifications

The history of fortifications in the Wessex area runs from the earliest times with the first beginnings of hillforts and fortified towns in the Neolithic period, through to the coastal defence and stop-lines erected in 1940 under the immediate threat of German invasion. It is ironic that the prehistoric fortifications with their massive earthworks are likely to last indefinitely with minimum management, while the brick, concrete and steel structures of 1940, built in a great hurry with poor materials, are already in an advanced state of decay and may soon disappear. The result gives us an unbalanced view of history.

The Neolithic causewayed camps, like the one at Windmill Hill near Avebury (W), were not primarily intended for defence since the banks and ditches are frequently interrupted by these 'causeways' and they probably have a ritual or social purpose. Population was sparse and there must have been less pressure on land and less need for defence. The first real defensive works appear in the early Iron Age and date from the 6th century BC, as successive waves of immigrants moved across Britain and found it necessary to protect what they had taken against the next invaders.

Almost all the surviving monuments of the Iron Age period are forts, which were progressively expanded and developed in complexity as the population grew and the external threats became greater, these culminating first in the arrival of the Belgic tribes after Julius Caesar's Conquest of Gaul in the 50s BC, and then in the period immediately before the full Roman conquest and colonization (which began with the invasion of Claudius in 43 AD, was carried through in the south-west by Vespasian in 44 and 45 AD and was eventually completed throughout England by about 90 AD). These hillforts employ a number of different features of construction, but it must be remembered that what can be seen now

is their last and most developed form with massive ramparts, ditches and outworks, while little visual evidence remains of the small simple forts which were the way many of them began. We get a very immediate impression of the collapse of a sophisticated culture in the face of Roman invasion. **Maiden Castle** (17, D) shows this clearly while **Hod Hill** (15, D) has a Roman fort built within the ramparts.

Those few forts which have had 20th-century excavations can usually tell a story of development over many centuries with continued reuse by clearly differing inhabitants. This is true of Maiden Castle, and also of **Cadbury Castle** (13, S) where the story moves forward beyond the Romans. Excavations of the Cadbury site have revealed continued development and use of this fort throughout the Romano-British period, with it refortified against the Saxon threat possibly as Arthur's Camelot, and then continuing in use even up to the 12th century. **Old Sarum** (19, W), another very large Iron Age fort, was totally revitalized after the Norman Conquest and became the home for town, cathedral, bishop's palace and royal castle, all within the ancient ramparts. This use continued into the 15th century (although only in its castle capacity, for the see and town were moved to Salisbury in 1219).

The Romans made some use of existing fortifications (Hod Hill being the obvious example), but generally built anew. In the 1st century AD the Romans built a fortress at **Cirencester** (5, G), and this was rapidly replaced by a large legionary fortress at Gloucester built to control the Severn crossing and to prevent the ingress of the unfriendly British tribes from further west. Once peace had been established, and the frontier forces moved away, there was little need for defensive works, and it was not until the end of the Roman period that town walls were constructed as at Cirencester and Gloucester.

Berkeley Castle from the south. Detail from a late 17th-century oil painting by Henry Danckerts. RCHME

The Dark Ages have left few monuments which are readily visible or visitable, but the linear earthworks at **Wansdyke** (22, W, A) are the largest and most indestructible. The Saxons have left little defensive work other than this and some smaller dykes (though the 'burgh' walls at Wareham (D) can still be traced), but their fortifications were slightly built in comparison to those both before and since, and their town defences have mostly been destroyed by redevelopment. The West Saxons, in their fight against the incursion of the Danes, based their defence on successful field battles, at Ashdown in 870, and decisively at Ethandun in 878 when Alfred comprehensively defeated the Danes under King Guthrum and forced their retreat from Wessex. These successes, together with his strengthening of the navy at its Wareham base, meant that Wessex enjoyed a more peaceful period up to the Norman Conquest than did some other parts of England.

The arrival of the Normans in 1066 led to the development of a social system in England dependent upon control by the Crown and the aristocracy, and which was administered from a castle in every locality, belonging to the Crown or licensed by it. Indeed **Corfe** (14, D) was a royal castle, while Devizes (W), Old Sarum (W), Malmesbury (W) and Sherborne (D) were built by Bishop Roger of Salisbury on the Crown's behalf at the beginning of the 12th century. Only Corfe and Sherborne survive to any great extent. Of the private castles, Farleigh Hungerford (S) is also largely in ruins but **Berkeley** (12, G) is still lived in and is the only one which remains virtually complete. **Nunney** (18, S) and **Old Wardour** (20, W) survive enough to be understood, for they are rather different. They both demonstrate the first beginnings of a new development, a higher standard of accommodation within what still appear, on the surface, to be strongly fortified buildings. Indeed, the medieval castles in the Wessex area have not survived well principally because of the area's strategic importance in the Civil War. Having been rapidly strengthened after a long period of decline, disuse, and often

ruination, many of them underwent siege, bombardment and deliberate demolition, often to a greater degree than they had endured in their period of ascendancy. As they were captured the castles were rendered unfit for further service by 'slighting', and stone robbers and natural decay took over. Bristol had a strong castle throughout the Middle Ages, which was besieged and taken by Prince Rupert in 1643 and then by Sir Thomas Fairfax for Parliament in 1644, after which it was destroyed, abandoned and built over, leaving only odd fragments now incorporated into the wholly misleading Castle Park laid out by Sir Hugh Casson in the 1970s. Some castles underwent complete restoration in the Victorian period, becoming major country houses of romantic medieval appearance: Dunster Castle (S), home of the Luttrells which features in Thomas

Hardy's *The Laodicean* is one such, and Sudeley Castle at Winchcombe (G), largely rebuilt by G G Scott in the 1850s, is another.

Towns also had their fortifications. The major towns were completely walled and these came into their own in the Wars of the Roses in the 15th century, such fortification only ending with Tudor peace after the battle of Bosworth in 1485. Bristol and Bath both had extensive walling, parts of which survive.

With the consolidation of England under the Tudors, and the development both of the Navy and more powerful guns in Henry VIII's reign, the coast was given greater defensive importance. The anchorage at **Portland** (21, D) was protected by a castle in the 1540s, and this was strengthened to meet the Spanish threat later in the century.

Berkeley Castle, great hall with screen. RCHME

Defence from invasion was principally the concern of the local militia who were grouped after landings to face the invading forces in battle, as at Sedgemoor (1685) after the Duke of Monmouth had landed unopposed. The real threat of invasion by Napoleon in 1803 caused great alarm in Dorset (graphically described in Hardy's *The Trumpet-Major*) and led to pleas for better defence, but it was felt that investment in the Navy was more cost effective than major coastal fortification. Nelson is supposed to have said: 'The French may come, they shall not come by sea,' and 19th-century fortifications concentrated on protecting the naval bases at Portsmouth, Chatham, Devonport and Portland, culminating in the chains of enormous forts of the 1850s and 1860s, of which Portland's Verne Citadel is the example in this region. These found virtually no use until the wars of the present century, when the last great scheme of national defence was built: the stop-lines constructed in 1940 with the intention of making German invasion so difficult that the defending forces would be able to regroup and repulse the invaders. There are still extensive remains of coastal defences in the Bournemouth area, strong points along the main east–west railway lines, and the Blue stop-line along the Kennet and Avon Canal, all of which have fortunately not been put to the test, but coastal erosion, development and natural decay are bringing about their return to nature more quickly than will ever happen to the Palmerston forts, or the Iron Age hillforts from long before them.

Cadbury Castle from the air. MOD

12

Berkeley Castle, Gloucestershire
12th and 14th century

ST 686989. On B4065 off A38, 4 miles W of Dursley

[A]

Berkeley is a castle which provides everything the visitor could want: a complete medieval castle lived in by the same family throughout, the scene of a particularly gruesome royal murder (your attention is directed to Marlowe's *Edward II*) in 1327 on the orders of the faction led by his wife Queen Isabella, and of a Civil War siege. It also has a particularly good Great Hall, fine medieval chambers with their original decoration, and a pleasant setting with pretty modern gardens.

The plan is a shell keep, begun in 1153 by Robert Fitzharding following a royal charter of Henry II. Externally the walls remain much the same as when they were built, complete with their battlements except for the large gap left by Cromwell in 1645. The attractive mottled appearance is the result of the mixed build of local red sandstone and hard grey tufa. The Norman origins of the building are immediately revealed by the doorway to the great staircase and the first-floor entry showing this to be transitional from tower to shell keep, a rare surviving type. Attached to the keep is a further circuit of walls, originally the bailey, but with the hall and other apartments built against them during the 14th century, and the outer castle walls pierced for windows as new standards of comfort and security gradually changed Berkeley from a fortress to a country house.

Ranged round the attractive inner courtyard are the Great Hall of *c.*1340 with its largely original roof and decorated 16th-century screen, and the private apartments reached by an oak stair of 1637. Particularly interesting are the Morning Room, once the chapel, with important 14th-century painted decoration and the Long Drawing Room. Among the humbler rooms the Great Kitchen demonstrates the adaptation of a medieval kitchen into one that continued in use into the 20th century. Of interest in many different ways, the castle repays a second visit as fully as a first.

13

Cadbury Castle, Somerset
5th–2nd century BC and 6th–9th century AD

ST 627252. SW of South Cadbury village, just S of A303

[A]

Cadbury Castle is not only an extremely fine example of an Iron Age hillfort, with four complete rings of ramparts, but it has been suggested that it may also have been King Arthur's Camelot. What we see today is certainly not the 'many tower'd Camelot' of Tennyson, but it does appear much as it would have done when the Romans first saw it in about 43

AD. The fort crowns a steep hill, 400 ft high, and is fairly heavily wooded. This, according to some Roman writers, is how British forts looked, though it seems hard to believe; but then we are more familiar with the severe bareness of Maiden Castle (17, D) and the other forts on the chalk, than those constructed on the more productive oolitic limestone. The ramparts, revetted by posts and faced with dry-stone walling, were reconstructed several times, and encompass about 18 acres with two entrances.

The identification of the castle as Camelot would depend in part on the credence given to Arthur himself. Perhaps he was the Romano-British leader who was victorious over the advancing Saxons at Mount Badon (thought by some to be at Bath, by others to be at Badbury Rings, 2, D), a battle which took place in about 490–500 AD and which appears to have given the beleaguered British a fairly lengthy period of peace. The excavations at Cadbury indeed proved it to have been a site of major importance at and after this time, and the finds included a great aisled hall but no round table. The fort was used by a number of widely differing peoples between 450 BC and 1200 AD, the longest span of occupation so far found in an English hillfort, apart from the very specialised uses at Old Sarum (19, W).

14

Corfe Castle, Dorset
11th century–13th century

SY 959824. On A351 halfway between Wareham and Swanage

[A] NT

The spectacular ruins at Corfe are the visible remains of a castle with a varied history, culminating in its deliberate destruction, or slighting, by order of Parliament, after a long and gallant defence by Lady Bankes on the King's behalf in 1645–6. The castle, which was garrisoned only by the Bankes's retainers, mostly women, had already endured a six-week siege in 1643 and lacked both stores and artillery. Even so

Corfe Castle under siege in 1643. A contemporary engraving. RCHME

it needed the treachery of Colonel Pitman within the castle to engineer its fall. Lady Bankes was allowed to keep no more than her life, the castle keys and, eventually, the ruins, which remained in the family until the whole Kingston Lacy estate passed to the National Trust in 1982, this time with the blessing and even the assistance of Parliament.

Contemporary illustrations show that, in 1643, the castle was all but complete, in its final medieval form of Edward I's time, with only the minor modernizations of Sir Christopher Hatton who owned it during the late 16th century. For the previous four centuries Corfe had been a magnificent royal castle, and despite the expenditure of some £368 9s. 0d. on Parliamentary gunpowder, there is still much that survives. There are curtain walls and the remains of a hall from the 11th century. The tower, probably built during the reign of Henry I, was modernised by Hatton, while the undefended residence, La Gloriette, was built for King John. The outer defences with additional curtain walls and towers, the great ditch and gatehouse were all completed by the end of the 13th century. Corfe is also associated with another royal defeat: Edward II was held prisoner here in 1326 before being taken to his death at Berkeley Castle (12, G).

15

Hod Hill, Dorset
3rd century BC–1st Century AD

ST 855107. W of A350, by footpath from Stourpaine

[A] NT

Hod Hill is a natural stronghold for it is a hilltop about the same size as Maiden Castle (17, D) but much more clearly defined, with double banks and ditches constructed on the north, east and south sides, while on the west side the ground falls so much more steeply that only a single bank and ditch were necessary. The fort was excavated in 1951–7 by Sir Ian Richmond and three or possibly four periods of construction were recognised, consisting of either additions to the defences or further strengthening of the whole fort. The south-east quarter of the fort has never been ploughed, and there are extensive traces of huts and storage pits indicating a large and permanent community living in the fort between the 3rd century BC and the final attack by the Romans in c.44 AD.

The Romans evidently thought this a particularly strong and influential fort for they annexed it themselves, building a fort of their own in the north-west corner, which they occupied until 51 AD. This is typical of the arrangments of the Roman army; the classic playing-card shape with rounded corners is divided into sections by the roadways running between the gates in the centre of the east and south sides, with administrative buildings to the centre and barracks in each corner. Parts of these internal buildings were still standing until the 1858 ploughing. This pattern can be seen repeated all over the frontier areas of Britain, but in this case the placing of the fort inside the Iron Age ramparts is unique. It was done to take advantage of the existing defences, to deny the use of the hillfort to the British, and to stamp the authority of Rome on the area in the most dramatic possible manner. This shows Rome at its most ruthless, 'veni, vidi, vici' in action.

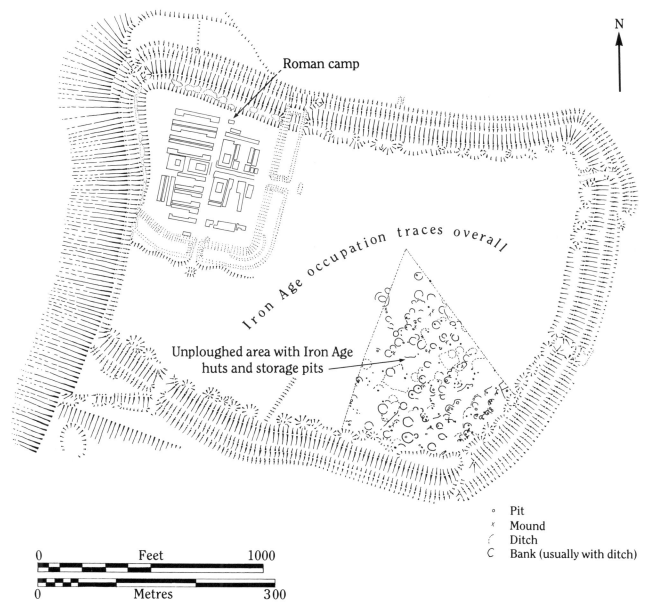

N

Roman camp

Iron Age occupation traces overall

Unploughed area with Iron Age huts and storage pits

∘ Pit
ˣ Mound
ſ Ditch
C Bank (usually with ditch)

0   Feet   1000

0   Metres   300

Hod Hill, hillfort and Roman camp (after RCHME). EH

16

Kennet and Avon Stop-line, Wiltshire
1940

ST 850596–SU 200630. Bradford-on-Avon to Great Bedwyn via Devizes, along canal towpath

[D]

A walk along the Bath–Newbury section of the Kennet and Avon Canal, or indeed crossing it at almost any point east of Bradford-on-Avon, reveals that it has a quality that other canals do not; it is, or was, a carefully organised line of defence against invasion and enemy occupation. Following the retreat from Dunkirk in 1940, and with the very real threat of imminent German invasion, a scheme for the defence of the south of England was hastily scrambled together. General Ironside, the area commander, devised a system with the first defence line on the shore (much of this, including the tank traps and dragon's teeth, has now disappeared through coastal erosion), and a second line, back from the coast, concentrating on the railway lines which follow the south coast fairly closely. Further back the stop-lines were

devised, one down the east coast and one right across the south of England. These were intended not for ultimate defence but to enable regrouping and to allow time for the civilian population to move out of the combat zone, all very much in the character of Churchill's 'We shall never surrender' speech.

The defence capability of water has been used throughout history in military planning and fortifications. It has a considerable impact on the outcome of campaigns, shown in Flanders during the 17th and 18th centuries and again in World War I. The one waterway crossing the south of England, the Kennet and Avon Canal, was utilised to form the basis of the defensive line called 'The Blue Line'. A large number of pill boxes and other strong points can still be seen, some bridges having two with another on a height behind, and they still bring a sense of unease to otherwise peaceful scenes along much of the length of the canal. The effectiveness that this narrow obstacle might have had against the Panzers must be left to the imagination. It is the best 20th-century defensive line in the country and makes an interesting comparison with the Arthurian equivalent at Wansdyke (22, W, A).

17

Maiden Castle, Dorset
3rd century BC–43 AD

SY 670885. Winterborne Monkton. W of A354, 1 mile S of Dorchester

[A] EH

Like all ancient sites, Maiden Castle is much more than it seems. The gigantic British fortress stormed by Vespasian and the Legio II Augusta in 44 AD still survives complete today, but, like any fortress, this was only the moment at which it stopped developing, and its history is really one of continued evolution and redesign from about 3000 BC up to the 1st century BC. It can thus be compared with Stonehenge (10, W), Corfe Castle (14, D) or Gloucester Cathedral (26, G), as a very major structure which became larger and more elaborate; then as with Stonehenge and Corfe, its major use came to an abrupt end, whereas the cathedral has continued to change and adapt in lesser ways up to the present day.

Maiden Castle began as a small causewayed camp of the Neolithic Windmill Hill folk with two lines of ditches round the natural hilltop at the

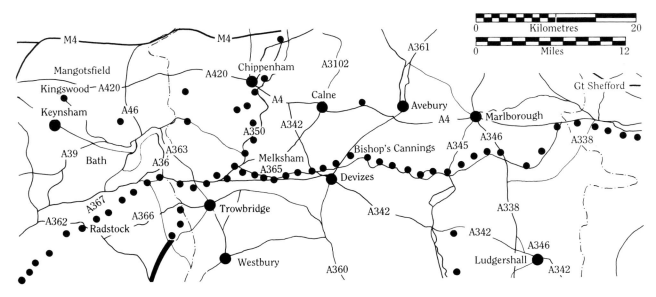

'Blue' stop-line, showing location of pill boxes in Wiltshire and Somerset. (After Henry Willis). EH

Maiden Castle. Reconstruction drawing of the town in its final form, viewed from the east. EH/PAUL BIRKBECK

18

Nunney Castle, Somerset
1373

ST 737457. In Nunney, off A361 3½ miles SW of Frome

[A] EH

Sir John de la Mere was given licence to crenellate (build a fortified dwelling) by Edward III in 1373, but it must quickly have become apparent that something rather different from a standard castle was being built. The late 14th century was a fairly quiet period for castle building in southern England, with the threat from France becoming dormant after Poitiers (1356), and strong castles did not become essential again until the Wars of the Roses in Henry VI's reign.

Nunney Castle was built as a strongly fortified manor, designed for comfort as well as security, and yet, with its uncompromising tall rectangular shape and deep moat, it still had the appearance of a proper castle. Sir John was a veteran of the French wars and this castle, more than any other in England, looks like an illumination from a contemporary French Book of Hours, with its cylindrical towers, once topped, it can be imagined, by the conical roofs and pennants which were common in France, but whose existence on English castles has always remained uncertain. The surviving tower (for there was once an enclosure on the north side) is the keep, standing four storeys high with the grand accommodation within, the hall being on the second floor. The essentially non-defensive nature of the tower is shown by the large windows in the long walls and it was the weakness in these that eventually led to the collapse of the north wall. Visitors fondly imagine that this was the result of an attack in the Civil War and perhaps a slighting (see Corfe Castle, 14, D) but not so. The wall will have been weakened by its Civil War siege, but it actually collapsed in 1910. The castle remains a dramatic and attractive one, and the adjoining early 18th-century Castle Farm, a smaller version of Mompesson House (Salisbury Cathedral Close, 46, W), adds greatly to its setting.

east end of the site. The camp was reconstructed on a much larger scale in about 350 BC, with a single large rampart and two gateways – a most unusual feature, as no other fort of this period has been discovered with more than one entrance. About a century later the camp was enormously extended to take in the whole hilltop, reaching its present size of 47 acres. The fact that it retained only a single rampart indicates a significant increase in population, rather than any new threat. From 150 BC through to about 70 BC the whole design was amplified, the existing rampart was heightened and two additional circuits were built with stone revetments and cores to consolidate their enormous structures. Additional elaborate outworks were also built at both entrances. The castle had now reached its final form as the largest and most strongly defended Iron Age town, the centre of the Durotriges.

Mortimer Wheeler's excavations in the 1930s have done much to bring the fort to life, although it is its dramatic fall which captures the imagination. The Roman ballista bolt embedded in a Briton's backbone, which can be seen in Dorchester Museum, is a powerful reminder of Roman intentions, but the British slingers must have done much damage too, and the piles of thousands of unused slingstones remain. No surface remains survive at all (ploughing of the camp was first recorded in 1610) but below the surface there are many indications of a large permanent population engaged in all the expected trades of such a town. Great numbers of grain storage pits and even some paved roads exist. There are also remains of buildings from the Roman period, showing that the camp remained in some sort of use despite the general movement of the population to Dorchester. The Wessex tribes put up a determined resistance, but Rome was too strong for them; and Maiden provides the best illustration of this change from one culture to another.

The south-east tower of Nunney Castle. RCHME

19

Old Sarum, Wiltshire
5th century BC–15th century AD

SU 138327. W of A345 1½ miles N of Salisbury

[A] EH

This large site has several aspects of importance but is included here as an example of the use and reuse of an Iron Age hillfort over a long period. The early Iron Age fort was a 30-acre area of hilltop surrounded by ramparts in a roughly oval shape, and this remains as one of the major Wessex examples. Following the arrival of the Romans with Vespasian's south-western campaign in 44 AD (see Maiden Castle, 17, D) the town and fort declined in importance. Although acting as the meeting-point of four key roads built as a part of the Roman programme to subjugate and colonise the area, there is little evidence of intensive use in either the Roman or the Saxon period. It may, however, have been the Saxon fortress known as Searisbying. This lack of evidence may be a demonstration of the archaeological methods used by the diggers in 1909–10, whose principal interest was the remains of the Norman period and who may have ignored other evidence. After the Conquest, a ready-made fortress at a strategic location must have been an attractive proposition, and under William I it was quickly colonised once more.

The motte and bailey castle built within one corner of the existing defences survives well, and this was improved in the early 12th century by the addition of stone buildings and facings to some of the ramparts. The foundations of the Great Tower and East Gate survive, as well as those of the palace built by Bishop Roger. All these were laid out for the public early this century and illustrate the display methods of the time. The consolidation of walling at this time has also caused problems of interpretation and repair. The interest of the site is completed by the ground plan of Bishop Roger's cathedral which greatly extended the

Old Sarum from the air, showing the Norman castle, cathedral and Bishop's Palace within the Iron Age ramparts. CUCAP

original church following transfer of the see from Sherborne to Sarum in 1075. The Norman cathedral in its final form is very large, 100 m long and 60 m across the transepts; but one can only imagine a church of magnificent appearance. Old Sarum was seized by Henry I in 1139, following Bishop Roger's disgrace, and the church lived uneasily under the Crown until 1217 when Bishop Poore transferred the see to New Sarum (present-day Salisbury), already a rising market town. The castle at Old Sarum continued in use until the 15th century, but, with both town and church gone, its importance dwindled away until

eventually little was left and almost nothing of this was visible until the excavating of this century once again uncovered its past glories.

20
Old Wardour Castle, Wiltshire
1390s

ST 939263. Off A30 2 miles SW of Tisbury

[A] EH

Old Wardour Castle is an attractive building, and it combines features in its

history and design which make it of unusual interest. It is an early example of the constricted combination of keep and inner bailey similar in some ways to Nunney (18, S) but unsophisticated in design. The first building, hexagonal in plan with an open courtyard, dates from the 1390s and was built for John, first Lord Lovel. The outer ring of walls was added in the 1570s. This type of arrangement with a central block allowed for more space and comfort and is eloquent of the less dangerous times of its building; the 15th century in England had been a troubled period, but once the Tudors were well-established,

29

Old Wardour Castle, the entrance front. MR

comfort could be accorded greater priority in the design and alteration of castles. In the 1570s Sir Matthew Arundel had the castle converted to a country house by the leading architect of the day, Robert Smythson, who was building nearby Longleat, and the classical character of his work is immediately apparent. The particularly fine decorative features of this period are the doorways, both external and in the courtyard. The new windows are oddly old-fashioned, with some false windows placed symmetrically for effect and actually with chimney flues behind them.

Two Civil War sieges in 1643 and 1644 saw the end of this house, the south-west wall being destroyed, and it was abandoned until Richard Woods incorporated it into a landscaped setting in 1765. Ruins had been a popular landscape feature since about 1750 and here was a genuine one, so little invention was necessary (in contrast to Blaise Castle Estate, 64, A). The pretty Gothic banqueting house is possibly 'Capability' Brown's work and shows how the 'idyllic' castle ruins were used as a setting for picnics and entertainments. One of Josiah Lane's grottoes was built within the bailey in 1792 to add to the romance of the scene (as at Bowood Cascade, 50, W). The transition of Wardour from fortress to country house and later to landscape feature is a fascinating one, and a visit to this lovely spot is always rewarding.

21
Portland Castle, Dorset
1540

SY 684743. By Portland Harbour, signposted from A354 at Fortuneswell

[A] EH

The Isle of Portland has two forts of quite different character and date which were built for the same purpose: the protection of the important anchorage in Portland Harbour where ships could shelter from south-westerly gales. Portland Castle is a grandiose name for quite a small blockhouse which was built during Henry VIII's reign at a cost of £5,000. A two-storey keep for accommodation and small arms is flanked on the harbour side by a gunroom in the shape of the segment of a circle, with embrasures for five guns within and a further five on the platform above. The available gunnery range of approximately ¾ mile allowed the protection of ships anchored near-in. The fort itself would be vulnerable to attack from the rear, if a landing was attempted, since the whole of the main armament faces the bay.

Henry VIII built a chain of such forts along the south coast to protect the various anchorages during the wars with France in the 1540s and many were strengthened at the time of the Armada. Portland never saw serious action beyond scuffles during the Civil War. During its later life it has been variously used as an ordnance store, a prison and even a private house and was finally given into the care of the State in 1980. In the mid-19th century its defensive role was taken over by a new fort built high above it (1857–81), the enormous Verne Citadel, one of the Palmerstonian forts built to warn off the French. There are chains of these forts at Plymouth and Portsmouth. This one, covering 56 acres, has particularly massive ramparts and deep ditches as the stone excavated could be usefully incorporated into the contemporary breakwater of the greatly extended harbour. The rifled 38-ton Armstrong guns with their 10-mile range gave a far wider field of defence, and this hilltop enceinte gives a field of fire in all directions. The new weight of shell carried by iron-clad warships meant that such forts were built with low profiles, immensely thick earthen ramparts, and underground storerooms and accommodation. It is now a prison

The gun platform at Portland Castle. EH

and only parts of the exterior can be seen, but there are several which may be visited, further afield, at Portsmouth.

22

Wansdyke, Wiltshire and Avon
6th–8th century

SU 045663–SU 195665. Various locations between Devizes and Marlborough, and S of Bath

[A] parts only

Wansdyke, or Woden's Dyke, is one of the few major sites of the Saxon period to be found in Wessex. East (W) and West Wansdyke (A) form part of a series of linear earthworks which appear in all parts of the country in various forms and, it is presumed, mark tribal boundaries of the post-Roman period of a definitive, if not really a fully defensive nature. The Wansdykes run in the east along the Wiltshire downs and in the west over the southern Avon uplands and are linked by an apparently undefended Roman road. This, and other adjustments which take account of pre-existing features, demonstrates its origin in the Dark Ages.

It is agreeable to associate the dyke with Arthur and the Romano-British rearguard, whose shadowy success at Mons Badonicus must have been nearby, but it could also be an early tribal boundary built by the West Saxons themselves. Wansdyke is a major feat of engineering and would have required much time and manpower, possibly enabled by the Arthurian success. It consists of a large bank, a ditch running always on the north side of the bank and a smaller bank beyond, the whole being 90 ft in width and, counting the gaps, some 48 miles long. It appears to

Wansdyke running east along the downs scarp at Tan Hill. MOD

incorporate several Iron Age forts e.g., Maes Knoll and Stantonbury, giving a stronger defence in parts, but the way it might have been manned and the length of time for which it was in use can only be conjectured. Of other such monuments in the area only the possibly 8th-century Offa's Dyke, running north from Chepstow between England and Wales and intruding a little into

Gloucestershire, is built to a comparable scale.

The best places to see Wansdyke are: on the minor road 1 mile to the north of Norton Malreward church, and at Stantonbury Hill near Stanton Prior, both in Avon. Also, in Wiltshire, a footpath may be followed for 4 miles, east from the A361 at Shepherd's Shore (SU 044663).

3

Churches and Cathedrals

The earliest churches in recognisable form are those of the Saxon period, and these survive far more commonly than many people realise, though they are sometimes altered beyond recognition. The characteristic features of Anglo-Saxon building, the long and short quoins, herringbone stonework, strapwork and interlace decoration, are a give-away when you can see them, but they are often concealed by later alterations or by render, and the true age of such a building may not be apparent until building work is undertaken. The Saxon church of **St Lawrence, Bradford-on-Avon** (31, W) was discovered in this way in 1857, when an antiquary recognised its early origins amidst the later alterations which were in turn brought about by its early conversion to other uses.

Saxon churches are commonly thought of as small in scale, and indeed many were, but not all. Bradford has been chosen as an example of a tiny two-cell nave-and-chancel church which is complete as built. It is contrasted deliberately with the enormous size of Norman **Tewkesbury Abbey** (37, G), built a century or so later. Deerhurst in Gloucestershire is a much larger structure than Bradford, and still has its bell-tower as well as sculptural decoration of the period. This Saxon church is said to be second in size only to Brixworth in Northamptonshire. Deerhurst also has a tiny Saxon church, 'Odda's Chapel', surviving beside the great one, and this too had its origin disguised in later building until discovery in 1885. An inscription dates it exactly to 1056, the only Saxon church with an inscribed date, and it is thus one of the group of buildings from the very end of the Saxon period, the reign of Edward the Confessor, when many of the surviving churches are thought to have been erected.

Many new churches were built following the Norman Conquest in 1066, though the majority of the smaller parish churches date from the first half of the 12th century. The greater churches, such as Tewkesbury Abbey and **Gloucester Cathedral** (26, G), were begun very quickly, for William I saw spiritual control as a means of keeping the Saxon majority in order. There was, however, no violent change from one system to another, few of the Saxon bishops were removed from office and one, Wulfstan of Worcester, was still bishop at the death of William I in 1087.

Many of the great Norman churchmen were also the temporal power in their area. Bishop Roger of Salisbury for instance was all powerful until his fall from grace in 1139. The Normans also encouraged the monastic orders to build in England, and the great churches were almost all a result of their activities. The familiar design characteristics of Norman (or Romanesque) churches, the massive circular piers, semicircular headed arcades, dogstooth and cable mouldings, highly decorated corbel tables, tended to be for the greater churches. However the commonest Norman type was the small two-cell parish church, nave and chancel without tower (hardly an advance on the Saxon ones like St Lawrence at Bradford-on-Avon), and many of these are still to be found forming the basic core of English parish churches, usually with added aisles, tower, chapels, etc., as the needs of the congregation changed. Today's parishes which retain their original Norman church must feel grateful to have a compact and solidly constructed building, which may well have fewer problems of maintenance and lower running costs than the large churches of the late Middle Ages, and the often poorly built ones of the 18th and 19th centuries. The area covered by this book, however, is not so rich in unaltered small Norman churches as some others, for population growth and the wealth from wool meant that many of the country churches were rebuilt on a much larger scale. Winterborne Tompson in Dorset is one such,

Gloucester Cathedral, interior of choir. RCHME

although the windows date from the 17th century, while two good examples in Gloucestershire are at Condicote and Clapton-on-the-Hill. The clues to the Norman origins of churches are the opposed north and south doorways at the west end of the nave and the general shape. The decorative features which most commonly survive are the chancel arch, quite often in a later church, and the surround or just the tympanum of the main door, as at Broadwell in Gloucestershire where a tympanum over the north door is virtually the only survivor of Norman date. The windows were often changed to give more light, but sometimes the rere arches (on the interior face of the wall) still show their characteristic arched outline or retain one deeply chamfered jamb.

In the cities, pressure from the growing population meant the reconstruction of most Norman churches; for instance the Norman abbey in Bath was totally rebuilt, but All Saints in Corn Street, Bristol, has Norman arcades and St James, Bristol, has most of the 12th-century west front complete with a wheel window.

Transition from Norman to Early English Gothic happened in the period 1180–1220 and is characterised by the arcades of now much slimmer circular columns with pointed arches. This feature occurs with surprising frequency, quite often just one arcade, with the other, if there is one, from later in the Middle Ages. As the Early English style takes over, the arcades heighten so that the arches appear taller and narrower, though the span from one pier to another may be no less than it had been in the Norman period. The piers are sometimes clustered round with additional columns, often in the distinctive dark Purbeck marble, contrasting with the white limestone, such as appears in great proliferation in **Salisbury Cathedral** (36, W) and at Westminster Abbey. As with the Norman churches the stylistic treatment is consistent, with pointed interlaced arcades along the triforium while the roofs are formed with more delicate rib vaulting also breaking away from the heaviness of the Norman work. This style predominated through the 13th

century but is nothing like as common as Norman work. Few of the small parish churches needed rebuilding, while the great churches were content to wait a bit longer before following a new trend. It is thus principally in the new building of the period that the Early English really prospered, as in the very special circumstances at Salisbury.

The 14th century saw the development of the style known as 'Decorated', of key interest to the Victorians centuries later when, under Pugin's guidance, it flowered again as 'Middle Pointed'. Bristol Cathedral demonstrates this style, while the cloisters at Salisbury are another gem of the period. The characteristic feature of this design style is the window tracery, while the much more elaborate lierne vaults are another element. (A lierne is a rib which runs not from a springer to a boss or from boss to boss, but from one of them to a mid-point on another rib and is non-structural.) The windows have by now become larger and the tracery is very complicated with cusps and trefoils, net shapes, tear shapes, or the slightly odd plate tracery where the openings are in the form of holes drilled in a flat surface. And yet, amongst all this elaboration there is also 'Y' tracery, or interlaced head windows which are extremely simple and yet date from round about 1300, this motif being much copied in the Gothick period of the 18th century. The other particularly memorable feature of the 14th century is the spire. There are few in England which are neither 14th century nor Victorian, the greatest of these few being that at Salisbury. Yet most of the cathedrals had spires in the Middle Ages; Lincoln had three, and old St Paul's spire was much higher even than Salisbury's. This area is not especially rich in medieval spires, and some, such as that at Yatton in Avon, have been truncated, but there are lots of good Victorian spires, such as the rebuilt one at St Mary Redcliffe in Bristol, and Christchurch, Clifton (A).

The area saw the greatest flowering of its church art with the coming of the English Perpendicular style at the very end of the 14th century. It is difficult to think of Gloucestershire, Somerset or

Wiltshire churches without remembering the splendid windows, the high vaults and wonderful timber roofs, and the many splendid towers for which they are famed, particularly in the woollen areas, the Cotswolds, the Mendips, around Taunton, and on the fringe of Salisbury Plain. It began with Gloucester Cathedral then St Mary Redcliffe in Bristol, declared by Elizabeth I to be the finest parish church in her realm, but there are many more of the highest quality to choose from. Among the great churches the most consistently Perpendicular is probably Bath Abbey, though it must be remembered that the vaulting is Victorian (a very correct piece, nevertheless, by Sir George Gilbert Scott). Increasing population and the great wealth of large parts of the area meant that there was once again scope for extensive church building, and the wool merchants sought to buy their way into heaven through it. The churches built include Chipping Campden, Cirencester and Fairford in Gloucestershire, Bishop's Lydeard, Crowcombe, Wells (including St Cuthbert), Huish Episcopi, Chewton Mendip and St John in Glastonbury in Somerset; St Stephen's, Bristol, in Avon; Beaminster in Dorset; and Steeple Ashton in Wiltshire.

The design characteristics of the style are easily recognised: enormous windows with the mullions sometimes rising through the tracery to die into the frame, fan and tierceron vaulting, panelled surfaces on tower arches and towers, and, most memorable, the towers themselves – particularly those with decoration in the yellow Ham Hill stone as at Huish Episcopi, and those with the filigree crowns such as at Gloucester Cathedral and St Stephen's, Bristol. But it is the Somerset group which is particularly famous and these date from the years on either side of 1500.

The Dissolution of the Monasteries in 1536 and 1539 brought to an end a specialised type of church establishment, the remains of which still survive as some of our most impressive medieval ruins. **Cleeve Abbey** (24, S) and **Blackfriars** in Gloucester (23, G) are the

St George Reforne. REDUNDANT CHURCHES FUND/CHRISTOPHER DALTON

Younger at Hardenhuish (1779) outside Chippenham (W) are four of the best, but there are plenty of others, among which **St George Reforne** (29, D) is especially complete and remarkable.

The late 18th century saw the beginning of the revivals: first the Gothick, and then with the 19th century, the Greek (**St George, Bristol**, 28), the Early English, and the Norman (**St Peter, Swallowcliffe**, 35, W). The Early English style was suited to the Commissioners' Churches, following the Church Building Act of 1818 – which at last responded to the threat to the established Church from the non-conformists and to the serious shortage of church seating – but most were built too cheaply to be successful designs. The 1820s and 1830s saw churches built in almost any style, although they mostly continued to be an architectural gloss on a rectangular Georgian box, and few were reconstructions of the past as thoroughgoing as **St Mary, Tetbury** (33, G) had been fifty years before. Thomas Rickman, a prolific church architect of the early 19th century, was the first to view Gothic architecture systematically and the terms Norman, Early English, Decorated, and Perpendicular were invented by him in 1811. This more academic approach began to lead to a much more deliberate imitation of the medieval styles, but any serious attempt to copy medieval construction did not begin until the formation of the Ecclesiological Society and the Cambridge Camden Society. These were the chief proponents of genuine Gothic architecture, and in A W N Pugin and William Butterfield they found the architects to match their ideas. Curiously enough, the archaeologically correct revivals of medieval architecture in the middle of the 19th century duplicated the sequence of the originals: first the Norman, together with Early English through the 1830s and 1840s, then the Decorated (or Middle Pointed) in the 1850s and 1860s (of which **St James, Kingston** (30, D) is a late example), and in the 1880s and 1890s the Perpendicular and Tudor – though by then academic integrity began to falter as the Free Gothic and Arts and Crafts styles appeared, and modern

selected examples of this type, and there is also a modern monastery in full traditional use at **Downside Abbey** (25, S).

Little church building was undertaken in the latter part of the century, and this trend continued in the 17th century which was so obsessed with political upheavals. Much of the building activity was the result of the collapse, or decay, of ancient structures, and it was on these occasions that the examples of 'gothic survival', the late Perpendicular

of the 17th century, appeared. A complete 'Gothic Survival' church, such as the one without dedication at **Low Ham** (27, S), is a rarity, as is the Wren type of church at **Newent** (32, G). Georgian churches are less rare and there are some particularly good ones in the area: Redland Chapel in Bristol by William Halfpenny (1743); Great Badminton (1786) (A) and Christchurch in Bristol (1786), both of which are based on St Martin's in the Fields; and the charming church by John Wood the

Wesley's New Room, exterior view with statue of John Wesley. PB

design: many of the leading architects designed for both Churches, while Pugin and the Hansoms were themselves Catholics. The free churches, originating in the 17th and 18th centuries, have a far more domestic look about them, and it was not until late in the 19th century that they threw off the chapel image and emerged as full-blown and often very imaginative Gothic churches. The early ones, however, should not be despised for their simplicity. An early meeting-house has as much interest and atmosphere as any Norman church, while Wesley's New Room and Whitfield's Kingswood Chapel in Bristol have more history than most Anglican churches. To begin with they were legally obliged to keep a low profile (the Quakers and Baptists in the 17th century built their churches to look like homes and attract no attention), but the best examples of these early types are found in areas other than our own.

23

Blackfriars, Gloucester, Gloucestershire
1240–1270

SO 830186. In city centre, off Southgate St

[A] EH

The 'mendicant' orders or friars were founded in the early 13th century in response to general dissatisfaction with the clergy for worldliness, and with the monastic orders for providing a service unrelated to people's needs. The Dominicans or Blackfriars first came to Gloucester in about 1239. The building of the house began almost immediately and was completed in about 1270 as home for some forty friars. The work of these friars was to minister to the disadvantaged, particularly in towns, but they also travelled out. They were unpaid, survived on charity and had no possessions, their houses being owned and maintained by sponsors who might be a lord or the town in which they stood.

The particular interest of Gloucester's Blackfriars is the complete

methods of construction such as reinforced concrete, as at **St Osmund, Poole** (34, D), were introduced.

The architecture of churches is by no means their only important feature: the ways in which they were furnished and used are also of great interest. Some mention of this has been made in the gazetteer entries, and I have no space to do more than say that fittings, furnishings, glass, organs, chandeliers, brasses, and memorials, all may be worth more than a passing glance, and a church cannot be fully experienced without giving these areas their due.

Churchyards too are wonderful places. Most of those in the Cotswolds

are worth looking at, and two can be particularly recommended: the group of early 17th-century bale tombs at Broadwell near Stow-on-the-Wold (G), and the whole ensemble at Painswick (G).

The churches of non-Anglican denominations also merit far more attention than can be given them here. They are represented by a major Catholic church at Downside Abbey (25, S) and the first of all Methodist chapels **Wesley's New Room** (38, A). The Catholic churches, built, as they mostly were, following the Catholic Emancipation Act of 1829, really came into the mainstream of Victorian church

nature of its survival with several rare features, and its history of adaptation and use. The church is on the north side of the quadrangular plan, and is complete in form, though not in extent, for the four arms are all truncated. The house was bought upon Dissolution by Alderman Thomas Bell who converted the church into a grand mansion, 'Bell's Place'. This survives externally but has been stripped out to display the church within. Only medieval fabric has been kept, and it has a largely glass and steel south wall, and a steel roof over the crossing, but the remainder of the magnificent scissor brace roofs are original and documented as gifts of oaks from royal forests during Henry III's reign. The other ranges were converted to a manufactory and have remained in light industrial use until the 20th century, but the south range is of great interest, also having the original roof, and internally the carrels or study cubicles of the friars, a unique survival of quality detail. This range is not yet open to the public. The west range, which poses an interesting conservation problem with the Georgian houses built upon it, can be seen from Ladybellegate Street.

24

Cleeve Abbey, Somerset
1200–1530

ST 047407. In Washford, ¼ mile S of A39

[A] EH

Of all the groups of monastic buildings surviving from the Middle Ages, Cleeve Abbey is the one that can give the visitor the best idea of what such places were like when in use. There are many monastic establishments where the church has survived through continued use, but the claustral buildings have been in part demolished, or subsumed in later building. At Cleeve the opposite has happened: the church and cloister have gone almost completely, while the rest of the buildings survive largely intact. This is, of course, the result of the sale of the abbey at the time of the Dissolution, in 1537, to a landowner who could use the buildings for domestic and agricultural purposes, but had no use for the church itself (see Blackfriars, Gloucester, 23, G and Lacock Abbey, 54, W, for examples of conversion for alternative use).

Cleeve Abbey, south range with frater. MR

Agricultural use continued at Cleeve for four hundred years, with the accommodation being successively downgraded as it became increasingly old-fashioned, ending as a simple farm on the Luttrell Estate. The Luttrells undertook some investigation and consolidation from the 1870s onwards, and in 1951 it was passed to the Ministry of Works. The surviving buildings are from two main periods: the 13th century when the Cistercians in general experienced a period of prosperity and expansion, and the late 15th and early 16th centuries when Cleeve, like many other abbeys, enjoyed a brief revival before the Dissolution. In the end there were no more than thirteen monks to pension off with the abbot, including John Hooper, later to be martyred as Bishop of Gloucester (1555) in the great purge of the new Protestant faith during the reign of Mary I.

Both periods show buildings of unusual quality and fine preservation. In the east range (built between 1200 and 1230) there is the dorter (dormitory) which survives complete, though the vaulted floor at the south end is a modern concrete reconstruction. The surviving details of the monks' cubicles, with their differing arrangements of

Blackfriars, Gloucester, exterior view showing north transept of church. EH

shelves, window seats and tiling, make it easy to imagine the place in use. In the south range, originally 13th-century but much reconstructed in the 15th, the magnificent frater (eating hall), with sets of chambers below, demonstrates the material comfort and privacy that the monks had come to expect in the late Middle Ages. The roof and the remains of plaster and decoration are of great interest. The west range (built between 1465 and 1530) contains the abbot's lodging and the cellar, but the former survived in use as the farmhouse into this century and has been considerably altered. Two other splendid survivals are: the 13th- and 16th-century great gatehouse and, behind the south range, the 13th-century tiled pavement from the previous frater – an extensive area of unusual elaboration which has been excellently preserved.

25

Downside Abbey, Somerset
1823–1938

ST 656507. In Stratton-on-the-Fosse, on W side of A367

[C] parts only

This renowned Benedictine Abbey of St Gregory the Great is a monastery and public school, with a wonderful church, and the full range of traditional monastic buildings of a high architectural standard. Founded first at Douai in *c*.1606 as a centre for English Catholic exiles, the community moved to England when an ex-pupil, Sir Edward Smythe, offered them a home at Acton Burnell, following harassment during the French Revolution. After his death in 1801 they moved in 1814 to the present site which had a Queen Anne manor house, now the school offices. Over the years this first building has been added to with buildings of quality for both the school and monastery. On the north side, the abbey church is notable for the commanding tower by Giles Scott (1938) and particularly the choir by Thomas Garner (1901–5) and the as-yet unfinished nave by Giles Scott (1935). Next to the church stands the monastery itself, which was designed by

Downside Abbey church, east end. MR

A Dunn and C Hansom and dates from 1872, extended in 1899.

The school by Charles Hansom (1854) is arranged around an open quadrangle the north side of which has the first school buildings designed by H E Goodridge (1823) standing next to the original manor house. The notable L-shaped block, mostly by Leonard Stokes (1911), was built as part of a much larger scheme intended to make Downside a major public school, but work was stopped by the First World War. It was finished off by Giles Scott in 1938. All is worth seeing but the abbey church is magnificent outside, and within has a remarkable sense of stillness and many rich furnishings of quality. A visit can give us some idea of what the now-ruined English abbeys were like in the days of their use, especially if the boys are on holiday.

26

Gloucester Cathedral, Gloucestershire
1089 – c.1450

SO 832187. In city centre

[C]

The complete rebuilding of Gloucester Cathedral began in 1089, replacing on a far larger scale a church which was only forty years old. It was consecrated in 1100 and most of this building survives today. However, the cathedral is included here for the work done to it in the 14th and 15th centuries, which saw the birth and flowering of the Perpendicular style of Gothic – the style which is more English than any other, for it was never copied to any extent on the continent.

Edward II, murdered at Berkeley

Castle (12, G) in 1327, was buried at Gloucester, where his relics immediately attracted visitors in great numbers. The income which resulted enabled the redecoration of much of the internal surface of the church, and the start of a great period of building: the first Perpendicular window in the south transept (1331–7) and the construction of the cloister completed in 1412, with its innovative fan-vaulting, displaying the principal characteristics of the English Perpendicular style. These cloisters must not be missed, not just for the vaulting (begun in the east walk between 1351 and 1377), but also for the well-preserved domestic arrangements for the monks in the north walk.

The great east window of fourteen lights was completed in 1350 and made the name of Thomas of Gloucester who went on to be the king's master mason. This window fills the entire east wall of the choir and appears to be a most unlikely feat of engineering. Although extremely strong it makes an amazing contrast with the tremendous weight of the Norman nave. The rebuilding of the cathedral continued with very little change in manner, culminating in the crossing tower whose magnificent presence dominates the close, the city and the vale. Dating from about 1450, the tower is 225 ft high, richly ornamented with arcaded and panelled decoration, and crowned by pierced parapets to accentuate the lightness and height. The west end is also 15th century, but the rebuilding of the massive Norman nave was abandoned.

Though Gloucester Cathedral led the way in the development of English Perpendicular style, its application of the latter was restricted to alterations and additions to what remains fundamentally a Norman building. To see a church built wholly in the Perpendicular one must look at Bath Abbey or, on a smaller scale, at Chipping Campden (G). In tracing the development of medieval architectural style it is interesting to compare Gloucester with the largely unaltered Norman church of Tewkesbury Abbey (37, G) and with Salisbury Cathedral (36, W) which was built in the Early English style.

27

Low Ham Church, Somerset
Early–late 17th century

ST 431291. Four miles W of Somerton

[C]

Low Ham is a rarity: a 17th-century church built wholly in the Gothic style, with no reference to the new classicism. That it held so firm speaks of the tenacity of tradition. It was particularly in rural places and in the private chapels of educational establishments and great family houses that Gothic persisted. Low Ham church was built as the chapel of the manor house which stood nearby. The house was demolished in the late 17th century and was replaced by a sumptuous new one to the south, coinciding with the completion of the chapel. This house too has gone, and, surrounded by greensward, the church remains in its strange isolation, among mysterious earthworks and without churchyard or village.

Built to a high standard, of local grey lias with yellow Ham stone dressings from the nearby quarries, the church is

St George, Bristol, interior looking towards the entrance. RCHME

late Perpendicular in character, and it is hard to believe that it was not built at least a century earlier. Both the window tracery and the arcades within are correct imitations of 15th-century works, and the 19th-century roof is the only major later alteration.

The visitor may wish to compare Low Ham's church with the manor house chapel at Wyke Champflower near Bruton (S), which is much more collegiate in character and dates from 1623–4. Low Ham's entirely medieval character contrasts remarkably with St Mary, Newent (32, G), where a 17th-century nave has been rammed unfeelingly into a medieval building.

28

St George, Bristol, Avon
1823

ST 582730. In city centre, off Park St

[C]

The rapid growth in the urban population during the late 18th century, coupled with the most undemocratic practice of pew renting meant that by 1800 free seating in parish churches had become grossly inadequate. One result

of this was that almost all new churches were designed with galleries for the poorer classes (see St Mary, Tetbury, 33, G), and galleries were also inserted into existing churches. The Church Building Act of 1818 provided for the building of new churches and gave the new Greek Revival style the opportunity it had been waiting for. St George's is one of the six Greek style churches designed by Robert Smirke, one of the leaders of the Greek Revival movement, and later designer of the British Museum. It is on a simple rectangular plan with a temple front on a high plinth, with a Greek Doric tetrastyle portico, but this is the altar end of the church and, most confusingly, the real entrance is at the far end. The tower – always a problem with temple type churches, for, of course, the originals had none – is a simple square one topped by a cupola. It is an extremely dignified and sophisticated building but tends towards the institutional rather than the spiritual in character. Inside, the church remains Georgian in feel, with a gallery supported on Doric columns and a flat ceiling. It was partially refitted by GE Street in 1870, and is now used as a popular concert room.

Sir Robert Smirke was one of three architects of the Board of Works who

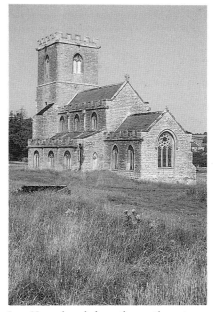

Low Ham church from the south-east. PB

produced designs for Commissioners' churches. The design used for St George was repeated at St James in Hackney, East London. St George was the only Bristol church in the first grant, but was followed by five others of which the finest is C R Cockerell's Holy Trinity at Hotwells, of 1829, although sadly the interior was destroyed in 1940.

29

St George Reforne, Easton, Dorset
1754–66

SY 686720. On Isle of Portland, at end of A354

[C]

St George Reforne exemplifies the Church of England as the Georgians understood and used it in both spiritual and physical terms. This cool, classical building illustrates the 18th century's love of order and precision. The appeal of this large church derives from the striking design by its mason and architect, the local Thomas Gilbert, the quality of the stone which comes from the adjacent Portland quarries, and the wonderful setting. It stands high on Portland surrounded by a broad sea of finely cut tombstones, many to drowned sailors, with views extending out over the quarries to the channel. Externally the church is simple and sculptural, cruciform in shape with a squashed dome over the crossing, and a west tower apparently modelled on one of those on St Paul's Cathedral, for which Gilbert's grandfather, a quarrymaster, had supplied the stone. The beautifully laid ashlar walling is enlivened by niches and panels with and without raised surrounds.

Internally, the arrangements now appear very unusual to a modern church-goer. In the cruciform space all the pews face the crossing where the tall twin pulpits stand, one for preaching and one for reading. Thus those in the choir have their backs to the altar, with preaching apparently taking precedence over devotion. The free churches reacted against this contradiction in the 18th century though the Methodists also used churches as theatres where preaching was accorded great importance. The difference lay in the free churches' belief in the equality of men before God. This particular aspect of the Georgian Church of England, the division of men into classes, continued into the Victorian period, though the Ecumenical Movement did bring about changes in church design and an apparent move towards a new form of piety.

30

St James, Kingston, Dorset
1874–1880

SY 955796. On B3069, 2 miles S of Corfe Castle

[C]

Kingston church is the ecclesiastical equivalent of Bryanston (51, D), as it involved replacing an existing building with something much larger and grander. The architect, G E Street, was not often given 'carte blanche', but he was in this instance, and the effect is breathtaking. He designed St James for the 3rd Earl of Eldon, who wanted to build a church for which he would be remembered, and to relieve the poverty of his tenants in a time of agricultural depression. The previous church was, and still is, large enough for the village and survives as the parish hall. The new church was built slowly and deliberately, using stone from Eldon's own quarries. It appears large in scale, though it is not particularly so, partly due to the high tower which gives the building such a commanding presence on the ridge above the village – the same sort of impression that the castle makes on Corfe itself.

The church cost £70,000 and looks it. The design is in the 13th-century style, with much French detailing as was currently the fashion with Street and other leading architects such as Pearson

St George Reforne, interior looking east, before restoration by the Redundant Churches Fund. RCHME

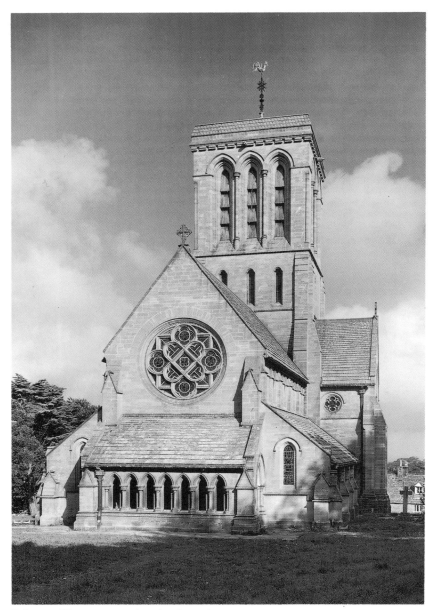

St James, Kingston, exterior view from the west. RCHME

and Woodyer. Both outside and in there is a progression in the quantity and quality of decoration from the west to the east end. The roofs progress from an open waggon roof in timber over the nave, through to a simple and then a more complicated stone vault over the crossing and the chancel. The nave arcade is in the manner of Salisbury Cathedral with attached shafts and stiff leaf capitals; and with small shafts framing the rere arches of all the windows. Much use is made of Purbeck marble as is only proper in this locality. The furnishings, all to Street's design, are also particularly noteworthy,

especially Thomas Potter's metalwork for the doors, screens and the most unusual pulpit. The windows are by Clayton and Bell.

Many Victorian church-building projects remained unfinished, but not so here. St James is one of the few buildings in this book which was completed as designed and then frozen in time, whereas most buildings have been adapted and altered to suit changing conditions. The church remains a monument to the ecclesiastical art of 1880: extremely polished and earnest but perhaps lacking something in emotion.

31

St Lawrence, Bradford-on-Avon, Wiltshire
10th century

ST 826609. In town centre

[C]

For centuries this remarkable survival was not a church, and its true nature was not recognised until 1857. It was then revealed as a complete and well-preserved two-cell Saxon church, dating probably from the 10th century, but possibly earlier. At the time of its discovery by Major Davis, the City Architect of Bath, it was a school.

The exterior is largely plain except for the arcading, and the vicissitudes of its life can be traced in the evident alterations to the stonework, and by reference to the photographs within the church. Its small size, but great height in relation to its area, its tiny windows and the lack of sophistication in the building as a whole make for a great contrast to the medieval parish church of Holy Trinity immediately across the road. But these are all strengths in this church and it speaks clearly of a different time before Bradford came to the relative prosperity and larger population it later enjoyed. Some Saxon churches, like Brixworth in Northamptonshire, are of a scale almost impossible to believe for the period; others, like Earls Barton in the same county, are very richly ornamented. The important thing about Bradford-on-

St Lawrence, Bradford-on-Avon, exterior view from the south-east. RCHME

Avon is that it is so unaltered, and can still give so complete a picture of a small Saxon church in use, with its plain surfaces, dimness and mystery; perhaps not so different from the temples of the pre-Christian period.

32
St Mary, Newent, Gloucestershire

SO 724259. In village centre, 10 miles NW of Gloucester

Newent's parish church has suffered a number of vicissitudes in its life, but all are instructive to those interested in ecclesiastical architecture. It is medieval in origin with the chancel and Lady Chapel surviving from the 13th century, but the most striking feature is the nave which, unusually for a small rural town, is completely urban in character. The medieval nave had collapsed in 1673 and the present structure dates from two years later, its urban nature due to its designer and builder Edward Taylor, a local carpenter who had worked for Sir Christopher Wren in London. He died in 1721 and is buried in the churchyard. With the assistance of local masons Francis Jones and James Hill, Taylor produced a more than respectable

church of the Caroline period. The wide-span ceiling, without pillars, covers a rectangular nave and fits rather uncomfortably across the medieval arches to both chancel and Lady Chapel, with a very wide pier between. The ceiling is supported on giant Ionic pilasters, four by two, and above that the timber roof trusses were related in type to those in Wren's Sheldonian Theatre in Oxford, but were replaced in 1906.

St Mary's has undergone changes which exemplify the life and times of almost every English church. Apart from the collapse and 17th-century rebuilding, the interior has been much altered. In 1675 the church was oriented towards the pulpit and given galleries on all sides. That there were tall box-pews is demonstrated by the high plinths of the pilasters. The Victorian Ecumenical Movement saw all this change: the long gallery was removed from the east wall, the high pews were replaced with low ones facing east, and even the plaster was stripped from the walls, anathema to a late 17th-century building. These insensitive alterations were mainly the work of John Middleton in the 1880s, but what remains is fascinating, and particularly unexpected deep in the Forest of Dean.

33
St Mary, Tetbury, Gloucestershire
1781 and 1890

ST 890929. In village centre on A433 [C]

The mid-18th century saw a revival of interest in Gothic decoration, inspired particularly by Horace Walpole's house at Strawberry Hill, Twickenham, built during the 1760s, and it was natural that this new use of Gothic design should spread to church building, for it was there that its true origins lay. Tetbury's parish church is an early example of the thoroughgoing use of the new style, here brought about by the necessity to completely rebuild the body of the church due to its decayed state. In Francis Hiorn's rebuilding of 1781, the medieval church tower was retained, but its rebuilding became necessary in 1890 and was carried out by the Gloucester architect Waller. As a result we now have an 18th-century Gothick body with a more archaeologically correct Gothic Revival tower from a century later. The 18th-century work is splendid. St Mary's is quite a convincing Gothic church, Perpendicular in character, and with

St Mary, Newent, interior looking east. RCHME
(*Right*) St Mary, Tetbury, interior looking east. RCHME

fine large windows, but the heavy transoms give away its 18th-century origins, for they mark the line of the internal galleries used in the Georgian period to provide more seating, particularly for the lower classes. This is all made clear in the very unusual and pretty interior: twelve slim clustered columns of wood, each with a central iron core, reach up to delicate fan vaulting and some of them are now curiously twisted. There is a full set of box-pews which are arranged as in a theatre of the period, being entered via lobbies from an external ambulatory which passes right round the body of the church. The Georgian pulpit is sadly gone but there are two lovely brass chandeliers of 1781.

The comparison with St George Reforne (29, D) is instructive, as it is with the full-blown Gothic Revival at Kingston (30, D).

34

St Osmund, Poole, Dorset
1904–27

SZ 044916. Off A35 Poole–Bournemouth road 1 mile E of Poole centre

[C]

This is an astonishing building, seemingly totally alien to its leafy surroundings in the Bournemouth hinterland. It is difficult to say if it is attractive, but it is strong and colourful. The style used is often described as Romanesque or Byzantine, but really derives not from the Franks but from the mingling of Italian, Early Christian or Byzantine influences found in the churches of Lombardy and the Veneto. It has mixed brick and terracotta walling, Lombardic decoration, a shallow saucer dome over the crossing and inside walls rich with mosaics. It is no copy, however, but an interpretation of these characteristics by one of the most imaginative of Edwardian architects. This is E S Prior's last important work and the overall quality of the building is certainly due to him, but its character and form was dictated by the already existing chancel of 1904–5 by G B

St Osmund, Poole, detail of west front. MR

Livesey. To this Prior added nave, transepts, crossing dome, and aisles – though the whole was not completed until 1927, long after Prior's death but to his original designs.

Structurally the building proved weak: the dome needed rebuilding in 1922 and the south aisle in 1950. Prior had chosen to build the aisles in reinforced concrete, an early and unusual use of this material. The interior is very fine, with sturdy square piers and barrel vaulted aisles, and there is excellent Prior glass of abstract design. In architectural terms, this church looks both forward and back, and is typical of the Arts and Crafts movement from which it grew.

35

St Peter, Swallowcliffe, Wiltshire
1842–3

ST 963271. Off A30, 6 miles E of Shaftesbury

[C]

The church of St Peter, Swallowcliffe, is as good an example of the Norman Revival as can be found anywhere. It is quite large and beautifully built, with

the great seriousness of Norman building enlivened by attractive use of texture and detail. The carvings are all of a correct Norman type though the castellated tower parapet strikes an incongruous note, as it was usually only a feature of churches in the late 14th and in the 15th century. Swallowcliffe is one of G G Scott's early churches, from the days of his partnership with W B Moffatt when they were busy with the austerities of the Union Workhouses (see Williton, 83, S). It shows that Scott had a thorough understanding of the qualities and details of Romanesque churches. This is a 'Norman' church built as new, complete and unaltered, with no suggestion of an organic development through time. Furnishings include a neo-Norman font, which presented no problem since there are many models for these. However, a neo-Norman pulpit needed imagination, and presumably Scott felt that if they had pulpits in the 12th century they could have been like this.

Almost unaltered since it was built, this church shows that the Norman Revival is not to be despised. It is a more interesting church than the contemporary and rather dull Gothic of several of Scott and Moffatt's churches in West London. There are two other particularly good neo-Norman churches

St Peter, Swallowcliffe, west end and tower. MR

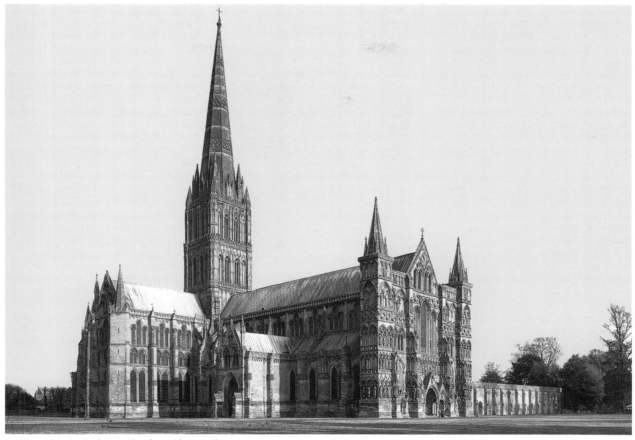

Salisbury Cathedral, exterior from the north-west. RCHME

in the area, which offer interesting points for comparison, the round St Peter's, Cheltenham (G), by S P Daukes of 1847–9, a conscious copy of a Templars church, and St Mark's, Easton, Bristol, by C Dyer of 1848, a late example of Norman Revival work, but very convincing.

36
Salisbury Cathedral, Wiltshire
1220–1334

SU 143295. In city centre
[C]

Salisbury is the most stylistically unified of all the English cathedrals. The Church wanted a fresh start for both

political and economic reasons, so a new town was founded, on better land and away from the king's temporal power (see Old Sarum, 19, W). The decision to move was taken at the very end of the 12th century, but the authorising papal bull is dated 1218. Bishop Poore laid the foundation stone in 1220 on his own land, and the cathedral was consecrated in 1258, an unprecedented building achievement. The consistency and symmetry of the building must be due to the very short time-span in which it was built, and presumably the limited number of architects and master masons involved in its design and construction.

The triple lancets, clustered columns, Purbeck marble shafts, the very sharply pointed arches and the long perspectives are characteristic elements of the Early English style and can be

easily recognised from Westminster Abbey to Beverley Minster, Humberside. The body of the cathedral was completed in 1266 with the lead roofing of the nave. The Chapter House, with its amazing central palm-tree column, dates from the end of the 13th century, as does the cloister, which displays aspects of the new Decorated style of building. The cloisters, England's largest medieval example, are anachronistic for there were no monks at Salisbury, and there are thus none of the usual offices which one might expect (see Gloucester Cathedral, 26, and Cleeve Abbey, 24, S).

The west front had a ritual significance in cathedral life (the doorway not being important since the main entrance has always been on the north side). It is wider than the building behind it and is the only element carrying figure sculpture, with a great number of symbolically arranged figures. The original arrangement is now lost and, though many of the figures are Victorian replacements (from the Scott restoration), it is still impressive. It has a clear stylistic relationship to the west front of Wells (S), and it is recorded that Salisbury borrowed iconographic books from Wells at the time of building, which it did not return for ninety years.

The tower, with its 180-ft spire, is 404 ft high, and the highest in Britain. It was probably built between 1280 and 1320, completing the cathedral. The spire was constructed on a timber framework which formed the scaffolding and which was then used to post-tension the structure; the base of the spire still contains the windlass crane used in its construction. The tower retains 14th-century iron cross-bracing, still in good condition. Sir Christopher Wren commented favourably on its design but added further ironwork. The effect of building the 6,400-ton tower and spire can still be seen inside the cathedral, for the crossing sank seven inches, the piers twisted and arch braces were added spanning the transepts as at Wells, but not across the nave and choir.

Tewkesbury Abbey, tower viewed from the north-west. MR

The present character of the interior, unusually open and uncluttered, is due to the restoration by James Wyatt 'the destroyer' in the 1790s. He removed the screen, rearranged the tombs, lowered the floor and limewashed the vaulting, thus accentuating the liquorice allsort contrast of the polished Purbeck shafts and the Chilmark limestone. Some of his work was undone by Scott in the 1860s, but these changes were also destroyed a century later and Wyatt's concept largely restored – a curious reversal in attitudes. In spite of this, Salisbury remains an unparalleled example of the Early English style of Gothic architecture.

37

Tewkesbury Abbey, Gloucestershire
12th century

SO 891324. In town centre
[C]

Tewkesbury Abbey has looked down on two historic battles. In 1471 the Battle of Tewkesbury, which ended in a rout actually around the abbey, settled the War of the Roses in the Yorkist favour. The second battle was a less bloody affair: in 1877 the Society for the Protection of Ancient Buildings, formed by Morris, Ruskin, Holman Hunt, Burne-Jones and others, opposed the proposals for a thorough scraping and restoration of the ancient fabric by Sir George Gilbert Scott. Their success spread far beyond Tewkesbury and was an important step towards today's system for the preservation of the national heritage. It has left us a very complete Norman church on a large scale, similar in conception to Gloucester Cathedral (26, G) but which has survived with more features from this early period intact.

The nave, probably finished by 1121 when the church was consecrated, has eight bays of tall, thick cylindrical columns. These appear to be greatly overspecified, as if the designer had had very little confidence in his structure, but they are immensely impressive and epitomise the massive solidity of the

Romanesque style. The west front has the same quality with its enormous recessed arch of six orders. This frames the Perpendicular window inserted in 1686 – a remarkable style for such a late date. There is still much Norman detailing on the outside of the building, though most of the windows are 14th-century Decorated. Internally the lierne vault over the nave, which dates from *c*.1340, replaced a wooden ceiling.

The roof was rebuilt in 1603, and the outline of the original roof structure can still be seen on the west wall of the tower. The tower itself is both high and massive, has the top three stages enriched, and is perhaps the largest and finest of all surviving Norman towers. The continuous blind arcading of the central stage is particularly fine; the battlements are a later addition. The east end of the church was much remodelled in the 14th century, but its Norman origins are still clear. There is also a wonderfully varied collection of monuments, including one to George, Duke of Clarence, one of the victors of the Battle of Tewkesbury, who, it is said, was later drowned in a 'butt of Malmsey' on the orders of his elder brother, Richard III. Tewkesbury has never really expanded beyond the confines of the medieval town (see entry 48) and the abbey, sited at its southern approach, still dominates the skyline.

38

Wesley's New Room, Bristol, Avon
1739–1748

ST 592734. In Broadmead Shopping Centre
[C]

The first Methodist chapel was begun here in 1739 by John Wesley and George Whitfield after the established church had closed its doors to them. The congregation quickly outgrew its home, and the building was reconstructed, and then re-opened in 1748, and remains much the same today. The design of the building follows the character of its church, being undemonstrative outside and plain but determined within. At the time it was politically necessary to present a low profile externally and the building makes quite a contrast with the lavish Methodist churches of the late 19th century, when Nonconformity could directly challenge the established Church. It seems to have been designed by the Quaker George Tully, the supposedly illiterate joiner/architect of the Meeting House which stands close by. The New Room was intended to provide space for a large congregation as well as accommodation for the ministers, and its design and layout provide a most effective solution to the problem of achieving this on a long thin site. The ground plan of the New Room uses most of the area of the site, with the galleries providing additional seating for the congregation. Private apartments were arranged along a hallway on the floor above, all supported on six Tuscan stone columns. An octagonal lantern passes from the roof to the ground floor, spilling light into the centre of the room. It is a simple piece of functional design (also providing light for the hallway on the first floor) and makes for a dramatic and attractive feature in the plain interior, reminiscent of the lighting arrangements in early passenger ships.

Wesley must have been involved in the design, which influenced the simple classical style used by the Methodist Church for the next century. The building is strongly evocative of the man and though he spent most of his time travelling the country on horseback, this is where his private room was, and it can be thought of as his home if anywhere outside London can.

Wesley's New Room, pulpit and reading desk. RCHME

4

Towns, Villages and Groups

The choice in this category is almost endless, for this region has always been blessed with a steady population, wealth from agriculture, and building materials suited to consistently attractive building groups. It is not an area of large cities, Bristol (A), with about half-a-million inhabitants, being easily the largest, with Bath (A), Gloucester (G), and Salisbury (W) of substantial size and Wells (S) really a very small place in city terms. All these are the homes of medieval cathedrals, though St Augustine's in Bristol did not become one until the 16th century, some time after the Dissolution. During the Middle Ages, Bristol was a larger and more important town in relative terms than it is now, and, for a period in the 18th century, was the second city and port of the kingdom, mirroring the importance of Cirencester (G) during the Roman period. All the other large towns in the area are principally resorts in origin, Bournemouth (D), Weymouth (D), and Weston-super-Mare (A) being the result of the mass seaside holidays made possible by the spread of the railways in the 19th century, though Weymouth had already achieved popularity in the 18th century because of the patronage of both the town and sea-bathing by George III and his family. Bath had been an inland resort during the Roman period, and from the 16th century became popular once more – though the curious aspects of the treatment for which people came were commented on by Pepys in 1668: 'much company came [to the Cross Bath] very fine ladies and the manner pretty enough only methinks it cannot be clean for so many bodies to go together in the same water . . . But strange to see what women and men herein that live all the season in these waters that cannot but be parboiled and look like the creatures of the Bath!'

Cheltenham (G) too was developed around its medicinal springs, though its principal period of expansion was later than that of Bath, being mainly in the early 19th century (see **Pittville**, 45, G). The Clifton and Hotwells area was also developed as a spa, and was really quite a separate town from Bristol until the mid-19th century. Its development pattern mirrored Bath to some extent, with the topography favouring crescents and elongated squares (**Lansdown**, 43, A) but it lacked the quality building stone enjoyed by Bath, and was built firstly of brick, and then of stone rubble rendered over. It shares architectural details, and indeed architects, with the longer established spa. The final large town is Swindon (W), which is a product almost entirely of the 19th and 20th centuries, though the remains of the old town, a small Wiltshire market town, do survive. The coming of the Great Western Railway (entry 102) in 1839 transformed the town, and designation for London overspill in the 1960s, plus the M4, has swollen it enormously in recent years so that it, with Bristol, is the centre of modern technological business along the so-called 'silicon corridor'.

The smaller towns mostly have their origins as market and agricultural centres. Some are of Roman foundation (though there was no continuity of use between the Roman and later Saxon periods): Dorchester (D), Cirencester (5, G), **Blandford Forum** (39, D) and Ilchester (S). Some are of Saxon foundation, such as Wareham (D), Shaftesbury (D), Frome (S) and Chippenham (W); some grew up round important castles like Berkeley (12, G), Corfe (14, D), Sherborne (D), and others around monasteries: Winchcombe (G), Glastonbury (S), Ilminster (S) and Wimborne Minster (D). It is interesting to see the relatively consistent growth arising from their different origins, with only the very special circumstances enjoyed by Bristol making it into significantly the largest and most important town in the region. There are also a number of towns which are principally ports in origin: Christchurch, Poole and Lyme in

Vicars Close looking south to Wells Cathedral. MR

Dorset, and Bridgewater in Somerset, all of which retain buildings of a nautical character (discussed in Chapter 9).

There are two particular groups among the smaller towns which owe their prosperity, and some of their physical appearance, to the woollen trade, especially during the 17th–19th centuries. One is in north-west Wiltshire and consists of **Bradford-on-Avon** (40), Devizes, Melksham, Trowbridge, Westbury, Warminster, Chippenham, and Calne, all of which can show good houses from the period. The clothiers' houses are of particular note in Bradford and Trowbridge. The latter has the most splendid of all, which is now Lloyds Bank and dates from c.1720, while Calne has a large square of good houses, and Chippenham has the rather hidden (but well worth visiting) St Mary's Street. All these towns have suffered to some degree from modern development. Bradford is the least altered and Trowbridge the most changed, while Warminster is very overrun by the army, as it is one of the centres for the Salisbury Plain training areas.

The other group of towns was more concerned with the production of the raw material rather than the finished goods. The sheep-market towns of the Cotswolds (G), Winchcombe, Stow-on-the-Wold, Moreton-in-Marsh, Fairford, Cirencester, Tetbury, and **Chipping Campden** (41, G) all have a consistent quality of building and a good survival rate for historic architecture which have made them into tourist and antique centres, their popularity increased by the growth of mobility and disposable incomes after the Second World War.

Many of the villages and smaller towns of the area are already renowned tourist attractions. These are included briefly here, to complement the places chosen for this chapter's gazetteer section. Badminton, Thornbury, Wickwar, Chipping Sodbury, Marshfield, and Wellow in Avon are particularly attractive and interesting and have groups of historic buildings including major houses and churches which are well worth seeing; Marshfield is the gem of these, but it is best visited in summer as it has the reputation for being the coldest place in southern England. Also,

in Dorset: Abbotsbury, Cranborne and Cerne Abbas; Gloucestershire: Newent, Blockley, Lower Slaughter, Lechlade, Newnham, Painswick, Frampton-on-Severn, Minchinhampton and Bibury; in Somerset: Stogursey, Stogumber, Dulverton, Montacute, (see also 55), Hinton St George, Selworthy and Dunster; and in Wiltshire: Marlborough, Hindon, Corsham, Biddestone, Castle Combe, Sandy Lane, Lacock (see also 54), Malmesbury and Uchfont.

The different characters of these places are due to the materials from which they are built, and the physical circumstances in which they exist. On the Cotswolds for instance the rare hilltop villages, supplied with water from deep wells and from catchments, make a contrast with the majority of villages in the river valleys. Thus **Stow** (47, G), Malmesbury, Condicote, Marshfield, Cold Ashton, and Aston Blank are all exposed sites, either on hills or on the open wold; while the river valleys are lined with villages in series named after the river and the churches: thus Coln St Dennis, Coln Rogers, Coln St Aldwyns. The Dorset valleys are similar, with the Piddles, the Tarrants, and, most common of all on the chalk, the Winterbornes with seventeen villages bearing the name in Avon, Dorset, and Wiltshire (a winterborne is a stream that runs only in winter as the

Fifteenth-century shop and house in Church Street, Tewkesbury. MR

headwaters of the chalk streams do). In Somerset the most attractive groups of villages are on the Mendips, and built of the grey limestone, like **Mells** (44, S), Nunney, Faulkland and Beckington, or in the area to the south of the county near Ham Hill where the distinctive yellow stone decorates all the local churches and has villages wholly built from it, like Hinton St George, South Petherton, Martock, and Montacute. Contrasting with these are the extremely dull and largely 19th-century villages on the levels which were developed only after extensive drainage. The villages in the Forest of Dean (G) are also disappointing; one mining village is very like another whether it is Coleford, Cinderford, Drybrook or somewhere in County Durham. There is little older development in the Forest, for settlement was forbidden for centuries, and most of the villages originated in groups of squatters' cottages.

Coming finally to groups of buildings, the ones which stand out are the church, manor and barn groups which are often particularly good: Stanway (G), Great Chalfield (W), and Toller Fratrum (D) are examples of this. The church is the obvious starting-place in the exploration of any village (e.g., Mells), and the best surviving buildings are often those grouped around it. This is not always the case, of course, as a look at any calendar with pictures of the area will demonstrate, Arlington Row in Bibury (G), Golden Hill in Shaftesbury (D), Lower Slaughter and Bourton-on-the-Water (G) being obvious examples. In a more urban setting it is in the square or the market-place where the groups are found – some enclosed and rectangular as at Stow-on-the-Wold, Minchinhampton (G), or Blandford Forum, others of a linear form like Chipping Campden, Moreton-in-Marsh (G), Chipping Sodbury (A), Dunster (S), Warminster (W) or Marlborough (W). Every town and village has at least one group worth looking at, a chance collection of houses, a planned suburb (45, G), a cathedral close (46, W), a commercial street (42, A), or a mill with its associated housing. My choice may not be yours, so you must look for yourself.

Blandford Forum, market place with Church of SS Peter and Paul and the Town Hall. PB

39

Blandford Forum, Dorset
1732–1750

ST 885063. 16 miles NE of Dorchester on A354

Blandford Forum is a small town with a centre of consistent quality and character which dates largely from one period. The town is older by far than it looks, but in June 1731 80 per cent of it was destroyed by fire, some 337 houses plus many other buildings. The subsequent rebuilding enabled it, as it says on the town pump by the church, to rise 'like the PHAENIX from its ashes, to its present beautiful and flourishing state', a state which it still enjoys today. Such catastrophic fires were not uncommon in the south-west, and were

partly due to the prevalence of thatched roofs which caught and spread the fire so easily; there was to be another of similar scale at Tiverton in Devon the very next day. Of course the greatest had been the London fire of 1666, and experience there demonstrated the possibilities and problems of such considerable rebuilding. Opportunities for major replanning fell by the wayside due to complex land holdings, and the necessity to rehouse the homeless rapidly. The Blandford corporation petitioned Parliament for an Act 'For the Better and more Easy Rebuilding' of Blandford Forum. This was passed in 1732 and contained important clauses for compulsory purchase of land, use of non-flammable roofing materials and the requirement to rebuild within four years or to risk loss of site.

The town was most fortunate in having architect-developers of the

calibre of John and William Bastard. The Market Place is the result of the Bastard's own landowning and family interests, the design of their own home and the Greyhound and Red Lion inns setting the pattern of red brick, tiled roofs and jolly baroque details. The very fine church and the Town Hall are also their design. Some significant changes in the town plan were brought about compulsorily during the 1730s, three islands of houses were swept away and thoroughfares widened, but there is still a squeeze in Sheep Market to the east of the church. All in all though, it was, and remains, a model town of the mid-18th century.

40

Bradford-on-Avon, Wiltshire
17th–20th century

ST 826609. 8 miles SW of Bath

Bradford-on-Avon is probably Wiltshire's most interesting town after Salisbury. Fanning out from an ancient crossing of the Avon, spanned by a fine medieval and 17th-century bridge, which retains its chapel and lock-up, the streets of the town climb the steep hills on either side. It is worthwhile exploring the riverside and the north and south slopes where the lanes, alleys and flights of steps lead past many attractive 18th-century houses, with walled gardens, and 17th- and 18th-century weavers' cottages. The north slope has Newtown, an area of late 18th- and early 19th-century housing,

Bradford-on-Avon, view from Town Bridge looking west, with Abbey Mills. MR

while the south slopes are a greater mixture with quiet corners and secret paths.

The wealth needed to make all this fine building possible came from the manufacture of woollen cloth. 'They told me at Bradford that it was no extraordinary thing to have clothiers in that county worth from £10,000 to £40,000 per man, and many of the great families who now pass for gentry in these counties have been originally raised from and built up by this truly noble manufacture', commented Defoe in 1724. Westbury House (c.1720) is the best and most conspicuous example of these clothiers' houses. In 1802 it was the scene of one of the first riots by the

Wiltshire shearmen, a short-lived protest against the introduction of new machinery.

The development of weaving into a factory-based industry is chronicled in Bradford by several water and steam driven mills. Abbey Mills, the tall block with gothic windows which forms the centrepiece of the view from the bridge, is the last and largest, built in 1875 by Richard Gane. The transport of the completed cloth to Bristol and London markets was greatly improved by the opening of the Kennet and Avon canal in 1810 which passes through the town (Dundas Aqueduct, 97, A, W), and then by the railway from Bath to Westbury which opened in 1858. Of all the

Wiltshire woollen towns Bradford is the one which has always been prosperous to a certain level, never so much as to bring about major redevelopment, as in nearby Trowbridge, and never so little as to bring decay and dereliction on any serious scale. The town is a microcosm of fine buildings from all periods, and of all types: the Anglo-Saxon church of St Lawrence (31), the magnificent early 14th-century barn at Barton farm, the Swan Inn (mid-18th century), the Town Hall (1855), the Post Office (1901 and 1936) and even K6 telephone kiosks (1935). Church Street has perhaps the best selection of quality buildings, with more beyond the bridge in Silver Street and St Margaret's Street.

Sheep fair in Chipping Campden Market Place, c.1895. OXFORD COUNTY LIBRARIES

41

Chipping Campden, Gloucestershire
14th–20th century

SP 151391. About 18 miles NW of Cheltenham

The Cotswold wool-towns of Chipping Norton, Burford, Stow-on-the-Wold, Blockley and Cirencester all have much in their favour, but in the end, they cannot compare with Chipping Campden. These handsome towns owe their existence to the successful agricultural economy and particularly the wool trade which produced the wealth sufficient to commission buildings of this quality in these numbers. Credit is due to the skill of those who designed and built them in the attractive Cotswold stone. Chipping Campden's long High Street with the two islands of buildings in the centre provides a wonderfully consistent procession of fine building from the 14th and 15th centuries up to the early years of the 20th century. Church Street, with its splendid almshouses, and the remains of Old Campden House, burnt to thwart the Parliament in 1645, culminates in St James Church itself, the most complete and splendid example of the Perpendicular style in the Cotswolds. It contains the fine brass to William Grevel (*d*.1401), 'the flower of the Wool Merchants of all England', who may have had a connection with the medieval house in the High Street bearing his name.

Sir Baptist Hicks of Old Campden House had a major influence on the development of the town; he built the almshouses, the Banqueting Houses and the Market House, and also the public water supply from the charming little conduit house out on the hill. In the 18th century the Woodwards, a local family of masons and architects, designed and worked on many buildings including early 18th-century Bedfont House in the High Street – one of the group of Cotswold baroque houses similar to St Edward's House in Stow, with its front articulated by giant

Corinthian pilasters. Like many Cotswold towns, Chipping Campden fell into some decay in the 19th century, but its fortunes were revived somewhat with the arrival of C R Ashbee and the Guild of Handicrafts, escaping from the mechanised 'civilisation' of London to a supposedly craft-oriented life in rural Gloucestershire. Ashbee restored two ancient houses, in which he lived himself: the Woolstaplers Hall in the High Street (1904–11) and the Norman Chapel House at Broad Campden (1911–19). The Guild workshops can be seen in the Old Silk Mill in Sheep Street. Together with F L Griggs (1876–1938) of Dovers House in the High Street, Ashbee was instrumental in bringing an appreciation of Chipping Campden to a wider public, and in preserving the architectural character of the town. Griggs was also responsible for designing the war memorial and the heavy wrought-iron signs on many buildings.

42

Corn Street, Bristol, Avon
18th–20th century

ST 587730. In city centre

Of all the commercial streets in the towns and cities of the region, Corn Street, Bristol, is the best. It is lined with Bathstone buildings enriched with excellent sculpture and carved decoration, and yet not overscaled as such commercial buildings can often be. Corn Street was always the main commercial street of the old city, rising from the quay up to the High Street. Luckily it was little damaged by bombing, although immediately to the east the devastation was considerable, and is now complete. Banks and insurance companies rub shoulders with clubs and commercial offices in this ancient part of the city, though some of the traditional commercial functions have now moved away.

The oldest building in the street, barring the partly 12th-century All Saints Church, is John Wood's Exchange (1741–3), a fine Palladian building with

Corn Street, Bristol, with the Exchange and the Old Post Office. MR

an internal, later roofed, courtyard. Behind the Exchange are the 18th- and 19th-century City Markets, still a lively and attractive area. Opposite this, the austerely classical Council House (Robert Smirke, 1824–7) stands next to Lloyds (W B Gingell and T R Lysaght, 1854–8), the most exuberant of the banks and a conscious imitation of a Venetian palazzo, with sculpture by John Thomas. Originally the entrance was in the centre of the five bays, but an extra bay with a new entrance was added on the left in Portland stone, this alteration becoming readily apparent when the building was cleaned in 1974. Further down the hill at nos 32–34 the National Westminster Bank (1855) is the work of the long serving City Architect R S Pope, and opposite this the mark of two interlopers may be seen: no. 43, the Bristol Commercial Rooms (1810–11) by C A Busby, chief architect of Regency Brighton, and nos 31 and 33 by Sir Edwin Lutyens, chief architect of the early 20th century. Some of these buildings have splendid interiors: the Exchange, the Commercial Rooms with its caryatid dome, and the three banks at 32, 33 and 55 can all be seen. It is also very pleasant to visit the first-floor coffee house to the left of the Exchange. This

Lansdown Crescent (right) from the air, with Somerset Place (left) and Cavendish Crescent (below). RCHME

these mellow lines of houses winding over the leafy hillside provide an architectural experience not found in other parts of the city, and yet one that is not appreciated by the majority of visitors.

44

Mells, Somerset
15th–16th century

ST 728493. 3 miles W of Frome off A362

actually projects into the body of All Saints Church where your meditations can easily be distracted by the clatter of cups and the buzz of legal chatter.

43

Lansdown, Bath, Avon
1780–1830

ST 748659. 1 mile N of city centre

The development of the upper slopes of Lansdown, above Julian Road, brought together the work of three notable Bath architects, John Eveleigh (Camden Crescent, 1788, and Somerset Place, 1790–1820), John Pinch (Cavendish Crescent, 1817–30) and John Palmer (Lansdown Crescent, 1789–93 and St James Square, 1790–4). This was the next stage of fashionable development following the establishment of the Upper Assembly Rooms (1768–71) and laying-out of the surrounding streets.

The south facing area of Lansdown, with magnificent views and healthy air, also proved treacherous ground for the

builder, for the slopes are steep and the ground unstable. Landslips caused the abandonment of Camden Crescent, and the east end, giving balance to the whole, has never been completed. Eveleigh's other crescent, Somerset Place, was caught by the collapse of the housing market in 1793 which was brought about by the war with revolutionary France. These troubles were familiar to Eveleigh, as the same things were happening to him at Windsor Terrace, Clifton, Bristol (A), which was also left unfinished. John Palmer, the City Architect, had better luck: St James Square and Lansdown Crescent were both completed just in time, while Pinch's Cavendish Crescent dates from the immediately post-Waterloo housing boom. The architectural quality of all these varies considerably. The Eveleigh designs have old-fashioned quirks like the five-column centrepiece of Camden Crescent and the segmental broken pediment at Somerset Place. The Palmer elevations may be considered rather long and flat, while Pinch's Crescent is just not terribly exciting, but taken as a whole

There is a story that the manor of Mells was little Jack Horner's 'plum' and perhaps this was so. It was certainly one of the richest of Glastonbury Abbey's manors and it is possible to believe that John Horner, who was Henry VIII's agent for monastic dissolution in the area, abstracted the deeds for his own benefit in 1539. The story goes that he hid them in a pie. Be that as it may, the manor came into the ownership of the Horners at that time and remained with them until the death of the last male Horner in the First World War (see Lutyens's war memorial in the village). Ironically, the house was to revert to

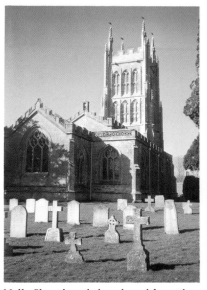

Mells Church and churchyard from the east. MR

Catholicism later in its history and, despite its direct access to the parish church, now has a private chapel in the garden. It is also where Ronald Knox undertook his translation of the New Testament in the 1920s.

With the long period of single ownership, the village has kept an extremely unified and largely unchanged appearance. The church is one of those Somerset wool churches most like the Suffolk equivalent, with a large and well-proportioned interior, and one of the best early 16th-century towers in the county – a tall, handsome specimen covered in delicate panelling. The churchyard is full of good memorials, including ones by Lutyens and Eric Gill and a nice one to Siegfried Sassoon. Don't miss the automatic stile at the north end designed by Lutyens, who was a friend of the Horners. New Street, leading up to the church, is a rarity – a medieval street. This was laid out in 1470 by Abbot Selwood of Glastonbury Abbey and retains much of the original fabric behind the 17th- and 18th-century fronts you see today. Round the corner is the Talbot Inn, also dating in part from 1470. Finally there is the manor house itself which dates largely from the later 16th century with additions by Lutyens. It is a mellow, much-gabled building with high garden walls, which forms a beautiful group with the church. For the best effect you need to go through the Lutyens stile and a little way up the public footpath through the field on the north side. It is well worth exploring the village further. The visitor should not worry about the explosions at midday for this is the centre of the Somerset roadstone industry and there are quarries all around.

45

Pittville, Cheltenham, Gloucestershire
1824

SO 954237. 1 mile N of town centre

Nature has not provided Cheltenham with the advantages of Bath or Clifton,

Pittville, the south front of the Pump Room. MR

and her Lansdown cannot be compared with the one in Bath (43, A) for it is built on flat ground so that the terraces can be seen only in conjunction with the one opposite. There are, however, some things which Cheltenham does better and more imaginatively, particularly the laying out of estates of villa residences around landscaped pleasure grounds. Pittville is one such estate, which, despite being unfinished, does demonstrate very clearly the direction in which respectable housing was going, and foreshadows the garden suburbs and estates which sprang up at the end of the 19th century. The town's common fields to the north of the High Street had been enclosed in 1801 and a large area was purchased by the MP Joseph Pitt. In 1824 he, together with his architect John Forbes, planned an extensive Grecian suburb around a park which was to contain a grand new Pump Room. This building, erected in 1825–30, sits on a little ridge above the park and overlooking the whole area. It is splendid both outside and in, and can be viewed from all around, showing it to be one of the best of such buildings. The now mature park, with lakes and lodges, is very good, but it is the open area of Pittville Lawn, fringed by Grecian terraces and villas, which, though never completed and only a part of the wider scheme, really lets you see what Pitt had in mind. The houses on the west side, along the Evesham Road, are of a later date, but there is enough of the original build here to show it to be one of the most agreeable residential areas in the country.

46

Salisbury Cathedral Close, Wiltshire
13th–15th century

SU 143295. In city centre

Bishops Palace (now Cathedral School): *c*.1220, *c*.1460, 1500, 1670–4
Malmesbury House: *c*.1719
19: late 17th-century
20: *c*.1720
Matron's College: 1682
Mompesson House: 1701–10
Wren Hall: 1714
Old Deanery: 13th-century
68: 1718

Architecturally this is one of the best and most unspoilt groups of domestic and semi-domestic buildings in the country, in a wonderful setting with Salisbury Cathedral (entry 36) and acres of green which were cleared and turfed by James Wyatt as a part of his cathedral restoration in the 1790s. Edward III granted the right to enclose the area in 1327, and some of the original wall survives. Many of the houses date at

Mompesson House, Salisbury Cathedral Close. PB

least in part from the Middle Ages: there are several undercrofts, and the Old Deanery is mostly 13th century, though well disguised.

The overwhelming architectural character of the houses in the close however, is of the period 1670–1740, with many very good examples of this particularly attractive style including the classic 'dolls house' type from *c.*1700. A personal favourite and the pick of those included in the list above is Mompesson House, a property of the National Trust, which is open to the public. This stands off the main green by the North Gate. The front is well proportioned in ashlar, in contrast to the brick of many of the other houses, and has the big hipped roof characteristic of this type of building. The date of this house is rather mysterious: it has a rain waterhead dated 1701, but the general appearance would suggest 1710 or later. It shows a distinct movement away from the earlier Wren-type houses such as the Matron's College of 1682 with its lower profile and mullioned windows. The interior of Mompesson House seems quite definitely to be of a later date, which adds to the mystery: the staircase, plasterwork and chimneypieces would appear to be more like 1740, which is quite a gap from 1701, and yet not perhaps long enough to merit a major refurbishment. Wiltshire is particularly rich in houses of this period (Heale House (4 miles north of Salisbury) with its Japanese garden is also well worth a visit), but Mompesson House has an unparalleled combination of architecture and setting. No. 68, once the home of Dr Heale, the first physician of the Salisbury Infirmary, and recently of Sir Arthur Bryant, is another contemporary house. Malmesbury House once entertained Handel, and has a sundial inscribed 'Life is but a walking shadow.'

One remarkable building has been missing from the close since 1790 when the detached bell tower, which was contemporary with the Cathedral, was demolished. It had stood 200 ft tall, but had decayed following use as a prison in the Civil War, and later use as an ale house.

47

Stow-on-the-Wold Square, Gloucestershire
17th–20th century

SP 192258. On A429, 18 miles E of Cheltenham

'Stow-on-the-Wold where the devil caught cold' is, at 850 ft above sea level, one of the highest towns in the south of England and certainly one of the most exposed. It is difficult to see why it exists at all in so windy and waterless a spot. The answer lies in its position at the crossroads of the Fosseway (entry 98) and the high road from London to Worcester, which was always an important travel and trading interchange. The Square, the main open space of the town, is huddled round with buildings to keep out the wind and keep in the sheep and cattle at the famous fairs. The space is divided in two by the central island of buildings including the Town Hall, dating from 1888 and designed by the local architect Medland. Despite its date, the 16th-century architectural character of this building is among the oldest to be seen: the houses surrounding the Square date from the 17th to the 20th centuries, though older buildings must exist behind some of these facades.

Architecturally the best houses, working round from the south-west corner are: St Edward's House, a fine Cotswold Baroque design of about 1730; the Cheltenham & Gloucester Building Society, a Queen Anne house showing the beginnings of the transition from

Stow-on-the-Wold Square, the south-east corner with the cross and the King's Arms. MR

the vernacular gabled house to Georgian Classicism; the old Rectory (now Stow Lodge Hotel); the run of houses round the north-west corner and the King's Arms Hotel. There are still five historic inns in the Square as befits its coaching past, and the King's Arms had the reputation of being the best inn between London and Worcester during the 18th century. The consistent quality of the buildings round this historic space, the gables of the 17th and 19th centuries and the flat-fronted elegance of the Georgian, give Stow Square a timelessness spoilt only by the constant presence of the motor car. But it has always been a busy spot even if not one to linger in when the wind blows over the wold.

48

Tewkesbury, Gloucestershire
15th–19th century

SO 893326. 11 miles N of Gloucester on A38

Timber framing plays a less important part in the vernacular building traditions of the area. There are plenty of minor examples in the Vales of Wiltshire, virtually none in Dorset and a few surviving town houses in Bristol. Only Tewkesbury, fortunate in avoiding major redevelopment, has main streets which are still lined with important and attractive examples of 16th- and 17th-century timber-framed gabled houses. These are interposed with good Georgian rebuildings, sometimes with older rear wings and sometimes merely a new brick skin in the politer architectural idiom overlaying the timber-framed structure behind. The town was very constricted by the surrounding rivers and monastic and manorial lands, with the result that the gardens and yards of houses fronting the main streets were developed, often as premises for the knitting industry. This produced the insanitary maze of alleys which was common in many towns, but in Tewkesbury it was not swept away in the 19th- and 20th-century slum clearances.

Abbey Mill and Mill Street, Tewkesbury. BTA/ETB

There are really only three main streets meeting at a cross, and almost all the historic properties are entered off them, access to those built at the back being through arches and alleyways. Luckily the planners have recognised the need to separate this historic core from modern development and the centre of Tewkesbury has survived almost intact. This is right and proper, for the town saw the birth of the Society for the Protection of Ancient Buildings in 1877 (see Tewkesbury Abbey, 37), but long before that, had prevented the demolition of the Abbey church after the Dissolution, when the townspeople bought it to be their parish church. In the 1970s the town saw another important piece of conservation: the 15th-century row of shops and houses at 34–51 Church Street were repaired and to some extent returned to their conjectured original appearance. One is displayed as a 15th-century house and shop. Otherwise it is difficult to pick out individual buildings; Barton Street, Church Street, High Street and Mill Bank are all lined with buildings worth looking at. There are fifteen historic

public houses, demonstrating the town's importance to travellers, and for the literary minded it is the 'Nortonbury' of Mrs Craik's novel *John Halifax, Gentleman.*

49

Vicars Close, Wells, Somerset
14th–15th century

ST 552460. On N side of Cathedral in city centre

A medieval terrace is most unusual and Vicars Close, Wells, is something unique: it is a complete medieval street of houses of a unified design character which, through single ownership, has retained its integrity to the present day (see also Mells, 44, S). The street comprises two vaguely parallel terraces of stone houses which flank a long narrow close, stopped at one end (north) by the Chapel and at the other (south) by the Hall. It was built as a residential college for the Vicars Choral of Wells Cathedral (lay brethren employed to

sing the Cathedral services) and dates from about 1360. These brethren were given a high standard of accommodation and a direct link to Wells Cathedral via the Chain Gate of 1459, which is one of the most beautifully articulated spaces in any medieval building, with a superb branching stair.

The terraces, thirteen houses on one side and twelve on the other, were originally identical but have undergone many superficial alterations over the years, mostly of a Georgian character such as the sash windows and the panelled doors with flat hoods. There are, however, many surviving original features both outside and in, and no. 22 was restored in 1975–85 by J H Parker, to what is thought to be the original appearance. The tall polygonal chimney stacks are all now restored and each house has a charming stone-walled front garden (four of which retain their original battlemented gateways). These two features were introduced in the 15th century, when the vicars insisted on a less smoky atmosphere and private gardens instead of an open paved court. The 14th-century Chapel, with its 15th-century library above, is very little altered, and a good example of a private chapel of the period; the Oxford college atmosphere is completed by the Hall which dates from about 1350. This has its original pulpit for readings during otherwise silent meals, washing place, fireplace, and a fine Perpendicular window and wagon roof. The whole Close is finished off by the entrance gateway with its four-centred arch. Passing through this gate on a winter's evening, one sees a peaceful scene which has changed little since the Reformation.

Vicars Close, looking north to the chapel and library. MR

5

Country Houses and Associated Buildings

The country house is perhaps the premier English contribution to the world's artistic heritage. An understanding of its architecture, the characteristics of its design and the way it was used in the different periods can only be appreciated fully through visits to as many different houses (and different kinds of houses) as possible. One must visit houses maintained as museums which have been frozen at a particular moment in time, and also those still lived in, where the character and original purpose of the various parts is still apparent. The National Trust has attempted to reconstruct this atmosphere as far as possible in its properties, while the Georgian house in Bath (1, Royal Crescent) even has half-eaten breakfast on the table! There is, however, no substitute for domestic use and this is where **Sheldon Manor** (58, W) is so effective, for it is a home, as are **Great Chalfield Manor** (53, W), and **Wilton House** (61, W), to a rather lesser degree, and there is room for both museum and family use.

The English country house really began in the 14th century. The peaceful lull in the Hundred Years War between Poitiers (1356) and the end of the century meant that new builders could turn their attention away from strongly fortified castles and build more comfortable manor houses. These were mostly for the lesser aristocracy and the new rich (e.g., wool merchants), who did not have wide landholdings or existing castles. These houses, with their characteristic hall and cross-wing form, with the great porch at the entrance to the screens passage and the oriel window to mark the dais in the hall, are typified by Great Chalfield Manor, while Sheldon Manor has a particularly fine porch of the period. There are very good further examples of this type in the area and the best are mentioned in the description of Great Chalfield.

These houses remained fairly consistent in design into the 16th century, but then a different type began to appear: first with the extravagant adaptations of the monastic houses which came into lay ownership following the Dissolution of the Monasteries in 1539, and then with the great show-houses of the Elizabethan period built by the wealthy courtiers, deliberately to impress. Most country houses called 'abbey' are examples of the first, but not all of course. **Lacock** (54, W) is one and Forde Abbey (D) another, while Wilton House is a third and Amesbury Abbey (W), though a genuine site, is a total rebuild. Other 'abbeys' may be the result of the 'picturesque' movement around 1800; there remains but a fragment of the greatest of these, Fonthill Abbey (W). The Elizabethan house, sometimes designed by Robert Smythson, the first really recognisable 'architect', and aptly called 'prodigy' houses because of their extravagantly rich and confused classical detailing, are represented by **Montacute House** (55, S), not the most elaborate by a long way but extremely homogeneous and attractive.

In the 17th century a new richness in interior decoration appeared in country houses under the influence of Inigo Jones. Wilton House is the finest example of this and shows the court or London style creeping into the provinces as it also did with church building during the period (see St Mary, Newent, 32, G). But there are many humbler houses of more traditional appearance (such as Sheldon Manor) in every part of the region, and the much-gabled, mullioned-window appearance which characterises them is repeated throughout the area, particularly in Somerset and the Cotswolds. The manor house at Aston-sub-Edge in north Gloucestershire, for instance, is completely traditional in appearance, and yet was the country home of Sir Balthazar Gerbier one of Charles I's

Gazebo at Montacute House. PB

Lacock Abbey, west (entrance) front. MR

premier courtiers, his chief artistic adviser, and a friend of Inigo Jones.

The 18th century saw the triumph of classicism in country house design: firstly the baroque, as at Chettle House (D) by Thomas Archer (1715) and Kings Weston House in Bristol (A) by Sir John Vanbrugh (1710); and then the Palladian style where **Wardour Castle** (59), Wiltshire's largest classical house, has been chosen, other examples being Prior Park, Bath (A) and Stourhead (69, W). This is the sort of large and very grand house which most people think of when asked to visualise an English country house – elegant, classical, with sweeping lawns and the evidence of ostentatious expenditure. This sort of thing has to be matched by equally ostentatious maintenance which is why Wardour, and Dorset's largest classical house at **Bryanston** (51, D) are now both schools.

The turn of the 19th century brought a new romanticism to moderate the austerely classical. The greatest Gothic pile, William Beckford's Fonthill (1796–1814), is sadly only a remnant in a still-memorable landscape, while the smaller but equally surprising Highcliffe Castle (D) by W J Donthorne (1830) still survives as a precarious ruin, though its future (it belongs to the local authority) is now more hopeful than it has been for years. The exotic side of country house building is represented by **Sezincote** (57, G), actually much less an imitation of a foreign style than it at first appears to be.

As the ranks of the wealthy grew in the 19th century, fortunes from the new industries joined 'old' money from land and agriculture, and gave respectability to the fortunes from trade which had

been the 'new' money of the 18th century and had paid for some of the houses of Paine, Adam and Wyatt and the landscapes of Brown and Repton. The new rich, in the best traditions of Mr Gradgrind, wanted the world to see where their money had gone, and their large ostentatious houses are represented by **Westonbirt House** (60, G), an enormous 'Elizabethan' pile which is now also a school. The increasingly elaborate stratification of life within these houses led to a proliferation of special rooms: a whole new suite for the use of gentlemen (billiard room, smoking room, gun room, library for naughty books, etc.), a servants' wing, a nursery wing and school rooms, and ever-expanding game larders, stables and bothies around the house itself. Toddington (G), Grittleton (W), Tyntesfield (A) and Batsford Park (G) are other examples of the largest kind of Victorian country house – only to be capped by Norman Shaw's Bryanston, which was built for Lord Portman with the profits from his London rents. During the 'golden age' before the First World War, there was the last great expansion of country house building. Then the increases in income tax and estate duty were

Sezincote, detail of the main entrance. MR

combined with a new social awareness and a collapse of landed rents to put the great houses into what appeared to be terminal decline. Many were demolished or given to the State or the National Trust. Some owners, however, held on bravely and the more recent increases in tourism and government understanding have favoured many new ideas for use and income generation, and have made the future for the country house more secure.

Each house and estate has other buildings, and these are often of great interest and architectural value. Four have been selected here from an endless variety of types, styles and periods. Ancillary buildings are often forgotten when visiting a country house, and perhaps will only be looked at when forced on one as with those surrounding the lake at Stourhead.

Displays at country houses in recent years have put more emphasis on what lay behind the green baize door, and it is often the kitchens and the stables which are most popular. The brewery at Lacock Abbey is another example. The National Trust has given a lot of thought to this, for the longer a visitor stays at a site the more likely it is that it will be appreciated and further visits made. The grotto, the prospect tower, the mausoleum, the obelisk, the column, and the triumphal arch are all part of the setting of a country house. Any of these may be a gem in itself and worth closer inspection.

50

Bowood Cascade, Wiltshire
1786

ST 978704. Between Chippenham and Calne on S side of A4

[A]

The Capability Brown improvements to the Bowood landscape are described in entry 65, but one structure does stand out as remarkable in its own right. The lake is held back by a considerable dam at the eastern end and the sluice allows this to overflow into an underground channel which runs to the head of a romantic rockstrewn little valley.

Bowood Cascade, with the water at half volume. MR

Bursting into the open at the summit of the rock pile the water cascades down, bouncing from the carefully contrived rocks so that it breaks up into long shining patterns of water in a 20-ft drop down to the stream below. When the water is in spate, on a sunny day with the light shining through the surrounding trees and catching the cascade, the effect is stunning. Among the rocks run little paths and tunnels giving many different views of the water from the top and the sides. It is, as can be imagined, very popular with children, being dangerous, dark and muddy; but looked at as art it is very clever indeed and not to be missed. The builder, Josiah Lane of Tisbury, was a famous grotto maker, using fantastic rock forms built of the curious volcanic tufa, and others of his build survive at Painshill in Surrey (owned by Charles Hamilton, the designer of the Bowood Cascade), at Old Wardour Castle (20) and by the lake at Fonthill. The one at Bowood, having the added dimension of the cascade, with both sound and sight effects, it is perhaps the best of them all. These fragile creations do not take kindly to heavy use, but remain valuable and attractive landscape features well worth preservation and repair.

51
Bryanston, Dorset
1889–1894

ST 871974. 1 mile W of Blandford Forum off A354

[B] holidays only

When Lord Portman wanted a new country house he chose the best architect and gave him *carte blanche*. He already had a house on the site; a smallish (i.e., not enormous) plainish (i.e., classical) and perfectly decent (i.e., a certain Grade I) house by James Wyatt dating from the late 18th century, but down it came and up went a wonder. Norman Shaw had built big country houses before, but this surpasses all the rest, particularly in the visible use of money which was clearly an important criterion. The house was to be the biggest and best of its day, the house

61

Bryanston, the Saloon in 1899. RCHME

that had everything. Its use as a private home, requiring enormous expenditure in every way, lasted only until 1928 and it has been a boys' school ever since. It is a key building in its way, Shaw's expression of the so-called 'Wrenaissance' which was to have so strong an influence on Reginald Blomfield and Edwin Lutyens. Shaw had only just finished a house for Lord Armstrong at Cragside, and he incorporated all he had learnt there in the way of modern domestic marvels

such as electric light, hydraulic lifts and improved sanitation.

Bryanston is built of red brick in English bond with Portland stone dressings, and gives the impression of a massively expanded late 17th-century mansion owing something to Wren, Hawksmoor and Gibbs. Of the two show elevations the garden front, with twenty-three bays, is perhaps the more successful. The interior is even grander than the exterior. It is centrally planned with a full-height saloon rising to the

cupola, and contains a heavy, late 17th-century style staircase and a first-floor balcony supported on Ionic columns. Cutting across the middle of this is a corridor running the full width of the house and wings, some 100 yds in all. A few classical fireplaces survive as a memory of the earlier house, as do the stable yard and service ranges. The overall effect of this house is powerful, almost monstrous and very memorable. Nothing like this had been seen since Blenheim and Castle Howard.

Plate 1   Stonehenge in winter. EH

Plate 2   Corfe Castle from the south.   SIL

Plate 3   Maiden Castle ramparts.   SIL

Plate 4 (*Above*) Montacute House, garden front from the park. SIL

Plate 5 Nunney Castle from the south with Castle Farm to the left, seen from the church tower. EH

Plate 6 Stourhead, with the Temple of Apollo. MR

Plate 7   Cleeve Abbey, precinct gateway from outside. PB

Plate 8   Salisbury Cathedral from the south-west. JARROLD PUBLISHING

Plate 9
Downside Abbey Church,
east end. PB

Plate 10
Tewkesbury Abbey
from the south. PB

Plate 11 Clifton Suspension Bridge from Clifton Downs. SIL

Plate 12 SS *Great Britain*. SS *GREAT BRITAIN* TRADING LTD

52

Goldney House Grotto, Avon
1737–1765

ST 576272. On Clifton Hill 1 mile W
of Bristol city centre

[A]

Goldney is not architecturally the most
elaborate of its kind, but no other grotto
makes better use of rocks and shells to
cover every surface, and this, after all, is
what grottoes are all about. This one was
constructed, and probably designed by
Thomas Goldney, a rich Bristol
merchant, as part of his elaborate new
garden. Built in 1737–9, and dated 1739,
it was then decorated slowly for ultimate
completion in 1765 when the floors were
laid by the leading local builder and
architect Thomas Paty. The entrance is
in the newly fashionable Gothic style
with pointed openings, but very plain
and built with a smooth ashlar face to
contrast with the 'classical' arches,
columns and vaults within, all encrusted
spikily with glittering rocks and gems.
These are stylistic contradictions, but
this matters not as the wonders of the
hall are revealed: the rock pool with
Neptune and the 'lions' den' lit from
hidden sources, complete with the
sound and movement of water and all

the sparkling effects from the rock
crystals or Bristol 'diamonds' on the
walls. Shells of all kinds abound as well,
including those of the giant Pacific
clam, some of which are said to have
been brought back by Woodes Rogers,
the pirate and rescuer of Alexander
Selkirk (Robinson Crusoe).

Also in the garden are the Rotunda
(1757), and the Gothic Tower (1764)
which is of great interest as the oldest
surviving steam engine house and was
built for a small engine to pump water
for the grotto and the canal. The grotto
itself can be compared with the ones at
Stourhead (69, W) and Old Wardour
Castle (20, W) while the Cascade at
Bowood (50, W) is a closely associated
form.

53

Great Chalfield Manor, Wiltshire
1467–1480 and 1905–1912

ST 860630. N of B3107 between
Bradford-on-Avon and Melksham

[A] NT

Wessex is rich in medieval houses,
having had long periods of peace and
agricultural wealth to build and support
them. One of the most perfect of these is

Great Chalfield Manor from the north. MR

Great Chalfield which, together with its
immediately adjacent church, great barn
and other subsidiary buildings makes a
memorable visual group. It is a
monument both to its builder Thomas
Tropenell, to the owner Robert Fuller,
and to his architect Harold Brakspear,
who altered it in 1905–12, and later
presented it to the National Trust for
permanent preservation. It displays both
fine original features and the insertion
of many early 20th-century features,
demonstrating contemporaneous
understanding of medieval houses.

The house is built to the normal
15th-century H-plan with an open hall
entered off a screens passage running
back from a porch, the hall being
flanked beyond the passage by the
kitchens and other service rooms and at
the higher end (i.e., behind the dais) by
a two-storey solar wing containing the
owner's private chambers. Many of the
external details, particularly the
windows, date from Brakspear's
restoration, but have been sensitively
executed, and the result is convincing.
Internally the screens, gallery, staircase
and some of the decorated ceilings are
all part of the restoration, for the house
had suffered alteration and division over
the years. The restoration is partly
conjectural and very attractive, and
shows the confidence of the time when
many a building was wrenched back into
the past, without the benefit of the
'conserve as found' philosophy of the
SPAB. Great halls of this type can still be
seen in use in Oxford and Cambridge
colleges. Other fine houses of the same
type and period are nearby South
Wraxall Manor (W) and Athelhampton
(D), while the 'Hall of John Halle' in
Salisbury (W) is a surviving hall from a
15th-century town house.

Goldney House Grotto: the entrance (left) and a detail of the interior showing the
shell work (right). MR

54

Lacock Abbey, Wiltshire
13th–20th century

ST 919684. In Lacock village 3 miles
S of Chippenham, off A429

[A] NT

Lacock Abbey is an example of the reuse
of a medieval nunnery as a private
house. The building is shown to the
visitor as an 18th- and 19th-century
country house, albeit a rather peculiar
one, and it is not until the visitor begins
the tour of the gardens, following the
terrace round the house, that the true
origins of the building are revealed. The
house is very odd in appearance,
especially on the entrance front which
has a two-storey hall and a double flight
of steps. It evidently has a *piano nobile*
with all principal rooms above a tall
basement in the Palladian manner (see
also Wardour Castle, 59, W), but is
equally evidently not a Palladian house.
The reason for this becomes plain when
'The Cloisters' are reached and the
visitor enters the medieval ground floor
of the building, which is not really

connected with the house above. This is
the almost complete and very high
quality survival of a 14th- and 15th-
century Augustinian nunnery: three
sides of a cloister walk with lierne-
vaulted roof, and opening off this the
sacristy, chapter house, warming house
and other rooms familiar from such
buildings. So Lacock gives a good
impression of monastic life (as does
Cleeve Abbey, 24, S), but provides a
particularly interesting example of the
adaptation of such a building following
its dissolution in 1540 when it was
remodelled for Sir W Sherington.

The house is also remarkable for the
quality of the early Gothic revival work
by the imaginative gentleman architect
Sanderson Miller for J I Talbot in 1754–
5, seen in the Great Hall decorated with
lively terracotta figures by V A
Sederbach. Much of the rest of the
interior is not particularly exciting, but
shows continued development in both
furniture and decoration as this rather
unwieldy building, arranged around a
large central courtyard, was adapted to
the 19th century.

The Talbots, responsible for the 18th-
century alterations, brought new

significance to the house through the
pioneering photographic work of
William Fox Talbot. The subject of the
first photographic negative, taken in
1835, was one of the south front oriel
windows which Fox Talbot had added to
the house five years earlier. The history
of photography is displayed by the Kodak
Museum in the great barn where the
first picture can be seen. The Talbots
were also responsible for the restoration
of the house carried out by H Brakspear
in 1900–10. In the stable yard there is a
complete 16th-century brewery, another
feature of unique interest. There are no
real gardens but the house is set among
attractive watermeadows and the village
of Lacock contains many good houses
and cottages, much being medieval and
timber-framed behind the stone facades.
Indeed the village of Lacock is one of the
finest in the region, having been
protected by single ownership.

55

Montacute House, Somerset
1590–1601 and 1785–1787

ST 499172. 3 miles W of Yeovil off
A3088

[A] NT

Montacute is a perfect Elizabethan E-
plan house built of beautiful Ham stone
ashlar from the nearby quarries. Its
proportions, decorative features,
window ratios and architectural finish
are all just right. Probably designed by
William Arnold, it is a little later than
the Robert Smythson 'prodigy' houses
like Longleat (W), or Wollaton in
Nottinghamshire, and does not share in
their overblown size and riot of
Renaissance detail. The visitor can
imagine living at Montacute, a quality
carefully nurtured by the National Trust.
The only major alteration in the house's
design was the reorientation in 1785–7
by Edward Phelips who wanted a new
main entrance aligned away from the
village. Remarkably for the time, Phelips
may not only have designed the changes
in character himself but also used
genuine Tudor features which he had
purchased at the demolition sale of
Clifton Maybank (D), a mid 16th-century

Lacock Abbey, south front with the Fox-Talbot oriel. MR

Montacute House, north front. RCHME

house not all that far away. These features, particularly the great porch, blend in well and show Clifton Meybank to have been far ahead of its time in the use of Renaissance details. Lord Curzon, who lived at Montacute in 1915–25, presented the house to the National Trust and they, as owners of Kedleston in Derbyshire, Bodiam in East Sussex and Tattershall in Lincolnshire, have the great part of the Curzon inheritance.

The 18th-century parkland setting at Montacute is worthy of the house, with c.1600 walls and wonderfully elaborate garden houses enclosing the area before the main front in what may be an interpretation of the fortifications of the period. Most of the garden building is contemporary with the house, but there are also sensitive additions by Lewis Vulliamy, one of the best of the 19th-century Jacobethans (see Westonbirt House, 60, G). Inside the house, the Long Gallery on the top floor, despite some alteration, has a new life as an outstation of the National Portrait Gallery and is lined with some ninety portraits of Tudor and Stuart notables,

of a variety and number no great house could have afforded.

Cranborne Manor (D) is another house designed by William Arnold; and Barrington Court (S) is a house of similar type in the area, while Longleat (W), Sherborne Castle (D) and Charlton Park (W) represent the grander type of Elizabethan and Jacobean mansion.

56

Monument to Lord Somerset, Hawkesbury, Avon
1846

ST 772876. 1½ miles W of A46–A433 junction at Dunkirk

[D]

A traveller on the M5 north of Almondsbury sees three towers crowning the Cotswold escarpment: the Tyndale monument at North Nibley, the local British Telecommunications Tower and, with its distinctive heavy top stage, this monument to Lord Robert Edward Somerset, one of Wellington's generals

at Waterloo, who died in 1842. The architect, Lewis Vulliamy, was an early Gothicist but he also employed the Italianate exotic manner and it is this that is used here. Close approach reveals a surprising design with Eastern overtones, a tall diminishing tower of 100 ft topped by a viewing stage with paired arched openings on either side, all supported on heavy brackets. The whole is constructed in the most magnificent Bath ashlar masonry which appears mostly as good today as when built and this, together with the unusual quality of the design, makes it a most striking building. It clearly bears some relationship to the nearby Lansdown Tower built by H E Goodridge for the eccentric William Beckford (this can be visited), which has a more classical purity of design and the same quality of construction.

The Somerset monument is all complete with surrounding walls and the Keeper's Lodge where tickets could be purchased for the ascent. The view over the Severn Vale is a memorable one on a clear day for the escarpment drops sharply right at your feet. Prospect towers were a feature of the 18th and 19th centuries and, although currently closed for repair, this one should not be missed. The Tyndale monument near North Nibley (G) can also be climbed, as can Alfred's Tower at Stourhead (69, W), while the obelisks to Wellington and Nelson's Hardy (near Portesham, D) are also worth visiting.

Monument to Lord Somerset, from the south. MR

Sezincote from the south-east. MR

57

Sezincote, Gloucestershire
1800–1805

SP 172310. 2 miles N of Stow-on-the-Wold, off A424

[A]

In one of the Cotswolds' loveliest settings can be found one of England's most outlandish country houses. Sir Charles Cockerell wanted an Indian style house to live in but, with true British compromise, he got a Georgian country house of the usual comfort and taste clothed in a different manner indeed. A mixture of Mogul and Hindu idioms, it is probably like nothing at all in India but is rather the Englishman's idea of what an Indian palace should look like. S P Cockerell's earlier Indian-style house was Daylesford (G), built for Warren Hastings (an Indian Nabob), but this is very tame in comparison. The main square block at Sezincote is built in orange limestone ashlar surmounted by a copper onion dome, this rich, exotic appearance being enhanced by the domed minarets at the corners, and the Mogul type decoration on the columns and over the windows. On the left is the sweeping arc of the Orangery and on the right the Tent Room, both graceful and

amusing designs.

The romantic landscape setting was designed by Thomas Daniell, a well-travelled landscape artist. Humphry Repton was consulted and may have assisted in the design and layout of the gardens which are in the 'picturesque' style, but with Indian-inspired features. The grotto, bridge, fountain and home farm are all very pretty, and the cast-iron bulls and Coade stone vases are further attractive features. The Wellington memorial, which is really the conservatory chimney, is a curiosity. Don't be taken in by the little Indian kiosk to the south east of the house, it is not an original feature but dates from 1953.

Sezincote is said to have been the inspiration for the Brighton Pavilion, the Prince Regent jealously driving John Nash to build a more peculiar building still, but there with the real glories on the inside. Sezincote's interior is decorated in the standard neo-classical style made familiar by Adam and the Wyatts, for example, at Dodington Park (G) which was designed by James Wyatt. One interesting innovation is the early structural use of cast-iron girders in the staircase, used in a decorative manner but still a peculiarity in a rich man's country house, for iron rather smacked of industrial building.

58

Sheldon Manor, Wiltshire
c.1282, c.1431 and c.1659

ST 887742. 2½ miles W of Chippenham, S of A420

[A]

Superficially Sheldon Manor appears to be medieval, having the same mellow stone and intimate feel as Great Chalfield Manor (53, W), but this impression is largely the effect of the magnificent two-storey porch which does indeed date from the later 13th century (c.1282). It is really too big for the house, which was largely demolished and rebuilt in about 1659, except for the 15th-century east range. The 13th-century house was built by Geoffrey Gascelyn, holder of the manor of Sheldon, and grants of royal oak trees from Chippenham forest are recorded for the years 1253–82. At that time Sheldon had a village immediately to the west and the outlines of the roads and house plots can still be seen in air photographs. The village had gone by 1582, presumably as a result of Tudor enclosure for sheep rearing, but by that time Chippenham had much increased in importance (the town charter dates from 1554). The Hungerford family held the manor for 260 years in all, though Sheldon was not their main house, and the 1659 rebuilding was undertaken by a tenant, William Forster, who demolished the hall and built a three-storey block using the old stone and incorporating the screens passage behind the porch.

This 17th-century work is of fairly consistent character but you can spot added 18th-century features if you look closely. There was a major overhaul in 1911, and many of the features date from then.

The interior of the house is also convincing, but here many of the very good features are introductions of 1911. These include all the excellent panelling, and the fireplaces, but not the fine 17th-century open-well staircase in the main range which is original. The 13th-century roof of the porch room, with its arch-braced coupled rafters, is an early type which survives in churches but is rare in domestic buildings, and it is unusual to be able to study one at close quarters.

This house has twice been rescued from near dereliction, first in 1659, and then again in 1952 by the present owners who are also responsible for laying out the gardens. Despite its varied history it remains a most convincing ancient house, charmingly shown as a family home rather than a museum. The gardens are very pretty and the food is excellent.

59

Wardour Castle, Wiltshire
1770–1776

ST 928269. N of Donhead St Andrew, off A30, 5 miles E of Shaftesbury

[B]

Wardour Castle epitomises the 18th-century English country house, the perfect model for Brideshead – a cool Palladian design set on a smooth south-

facing hillside with a landscape setting designed by Richard Woods in the style of Capability Brown. The fine ruins of Old Wardour Castle (20, W) stand beside the lake; and there is a magnificent Catholic chapel, for the new house was built for the Arundels, one of England's premier Catholic families.

Externally the design of the house lacks sparkle for it is in James Paine's late, and rather flat manner, when Palladian was really rather *déjà vu* and the *cognoscenti* were going to Robert Adam for the truly fashionable designs. The house was designed to face north, but was turned round when built and thus the garden and entrance fronts are reversed. The rusticated basement (or ground floor) carries the *piano nobile*, with all the principal rooms, and the centre bays of the block are set forward and framed by Corinthian columns. In the Italian originals the principal floor would be approached by an external staircase, but in the colder climate of England this must be achieved internally, and was often a problem for the designer. At Wardour Paine overcomes this with a magnificent

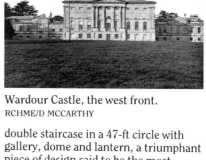

Wardour Castle, the west front.
RCHME/D MCCARTHY

double staircase in a 47-ft circle with gallery, dome and lantern, a triumphant piece of design said to be the most successful in this country. Surprisingly the scale is not quite as big as one feels it should be, but perhaps truer to the villa original than a larger staircase would have been.

The interior is otherwise fairly restrained. Sir John Soane also worked here and there is a characteristic saucer dome in the Reading room, while the Boudoir is decorated in the Etruscan manner first invented by Robert Adam. The chapel, which is attached to the house and forms one of the balancing wings, is truly splendid with its groin-vaulted interior lined with composite pilasters. The apse was added by Soane in 1789 and is more successful inside than out because it damages the pavilion's symmetry. The chapel also has an important set of Italian furnishings, paintings and vestments producing a rich and varied interior of a quality unusual outside London.

60

Westonbirt House, Gloucestershire
1863–1870

ST 897864. 3 miles SW of Tetbury, off A433

[D]

As an example of a sumptuous Victorian country house with all its trimmings Westonbirt is hard to better. It has an extremely elaborate exterior, a very complete interior, large gardens, a deer park with fine trees, entrance lodges almost as good as the house and, across

Sheldon Manor. CL

Westonbirt House, the south front from the churchyard. MR

the road, the finest arboretum in the country (see entry 71), though the latter is now the property of the Forestry Commission.

Built by Lewis Vulliamy for R S Holford, in the style of an Elizabethan 'prodigy house' such as Wollaton or Longleat, it is a riot of decorative stonework in Bathstone ashlar of the highest quality, with all the wall surfaces broken up with projections, indentations, strapwork and a profusion of the classical orders, while the roofline is spiky and varied with towers, obelisks and chimneys. The whole is not necessarily to your taste but it has an undeniable presence in the 18th-century landscaped park, with the towers topping the oaks and chestnuts. The garden front and the magnificent Italian gardens with their long lines of stone balustrading can easily be admired from the churchyard. The Italian garden is a much larger example than the one at Bowood (65, W) and was possibly designed by Holford himself, with the architectural embellishment by Vulliamy and H S Hamlen.

The interior, which is curiously more rogue classical than Elizabethan, is also richly finished and well preserved, despite its long use as a school. The rooms are arranged on the main floors round the central, top-lit hall-cum-saloon and have high quality joinery, original silk and leather wall coverings and painted decoration in the main bedrooms. The staircase too is a magnificent one.

Westonbirt also clearly demonstrates the careful planning and arrangement of such houses reflecting the social

stratification of the period and was built with every convenience of Victorian technology. It is a memorable ensemble, which can be admired in microcosm in the entrance lodges and gates probably designed by the same architect as a prototype – they date from 1853, ten years before work began on the house itself.

61

Wilton House, Wiltshire
16th–19th century

SU 099310. S of A30 near Wilton town centre

[A]

Wilton House is one of the great architectural puzzles, beloved of historians, where the ground constantly shifts and you can believe almost what you like. It originated as a nunnery (but there is little to remind you of this), was granted to the Pembrokes in 1544, and remains with them today. The main front has the three-storey entrance tower of the Tudor mansion, and the courtyard plan is still evident, but what is really important is the garden front, built in Charles I's reign, and the suite of grand reception rooms behind it, the

Double and Single Cube rooms being the major survival of the Caroline interior.

The south range (1636–40) appears to have been designed by Isaac de Caus on the recommendation, and with the assistance of, Inigo Jones. Though only a half of what was originally intended, it proved to be extremely influential in the 18th century when its basic design characteristics, especially the corner towers, were copied at such houses as Hagley (West Midlands); Lydiard Tregoze (W) and Combe Bank (Kent). This range was gutted by fire soon after completion (1647–8), though the extent of the damage remains conjectural, and its present interior (c.1650) is the work of Inigo Jones and his assistant and son-in-law John Webb. The Double Cube (60 ft × 30 ft × 30 ft) is breathtaking. It is a very richly modelled frame for the Pembroke family portraits by Anthony Van Dyke; and the large family group dates from c.1634. All the carved decoration, the swags of fruit (referred to by Sir William Chambers as 'bunches of turnips'), and the ceiling paintings, add to the splendid effect. It has recently been suggested that some of the decoration at least dates from the Edwardian alterations. The large family group, for instance, probably hung in

Wilton House, the south front. RCHME

the Pembrokes' London house and was not at Wilton in the 1650s.

The house does not end here, though. Further features were added in 1801–11 by James Wyatt, who pulled down 16th-century ranges to make room for the Gothic cloister, which is thin but pretty, as is his hall. The triumphal arch by Chambers makes a splendid entrance to the courtyard. It was an eyecatcher put up in the park in 1759, but Wyatt moved it to where it now is in 1800; and there are important garden buildings including the famous Palladian bridge of 1737 designed by the architect 9th Earl together with Roger Morris and copied several times, as at Stowe in Bucks, Prior Park (A), Hagley in W. Midlands and Amesbury (W), and the grotto designed by de Caus. Wilton is a house of joint efforts, where the dividing lines are often difficult to see, but it is certainly not dull, nor does it merit Pepys's 'the situation I do not much like, nor the house promise much' – but then he was not allowed in.

62

Worcester Lodge, Badminton Park, Gloucestershire
1746

ST 872811. 7 miles SW of Tetbury on A433

[D]

This is a most sophisticated architectural statement, a building without real use, built only for a rich man's pleasure, designed very expensively and to the highest degree of finish both inside and out. It forms the lodge and gateway to a back drive of Badminton House, the Three Mile Drive to the Worcester Road, but is really intended as a picnic house. The upper dining room under the dome is for comfortable midday meals, protected from the elements, for the hunting Dukes of Beaufort. The Lodge exemplifies all such estate buildings – in

Worcester Lodge from the north. PB

an area and from a century rich in them – and the men prepared to build them. Externally it demonstrates wealth, power and taste to the passer-by on the high road, a private world from which they are excluded. The wealthy used the rooms above, and below, in the pyramids on either side, were the gatekeepers whose duty it was to service the pleasure of the mighty. As a piece of architecture it is of exceptional splendour. Clearly moving on from the monumental style of garden building perfected by Vanbrugh and Hawksmoor at Blenheim

and Castle Howard, William Kent here improved the massive sculptural qualities of those by mixing simple geometry with richly textured surfaces, the rusticated and vermiculated stonework of the Palladians. The interior is richer still, a cantilevered, moulded stone stair leads to the upper room, which Kent decorated with plasterwork depicting fruit and flowers of the four seasons. This is a wonderfully attractive and mysterious structure, which appears as if built from a set of child's building blocks.

6

Parks and Gardens

Flower gardens have always been associated with English houses of every scale and quality, and herbs and vegetables too have played their part from monastery to cottage. There are few visible remains of early gardens in England, though some full-scale reconstructions, such as the Roman palace garden at Fishbourne in Hampshire, have been attempted, and it is not really until the 16th century, when the formal garden designs began to involve considerable earthworks, that their survival as relics is really significant. A study of Tudor and Stuart earthwork gardens in the Northamptonshire and Cambridgeshire areas has shown just how widespread such gardens were. Every significant house of the period could be expected to have one, and further fieldwork, and especially air photography, will reveal more. The formal style with decorative parterres and knot gardens was to find favour again in the early Victorian period, but at the end of the 17th century it began to spread beyond the immediate environs of the house and to encompass the landscape around. The parks surrounding Elizabethan houses had been deer parks in a semi-natural state, like the small remaining one at Magdalen College, Oxford. With the reign of Charles II, who had lived in France during his exile, the idea of artificially designed landscapes was brought to England. The French manner of very large-scale editing of one's surroundings, as at Versailles and Vaux-le-Vicomte, and brought to perfection by Louis XIV's gardener Le Nôtre, was not suited to England's smaller-scale environments, and only a few really large schemes were attempted; others followed the more inward-looking designs inspired by Dutch gardening and introduced by William and Mary. Le Nôtre himself advised Charles II over St James's Park and Greenwich Park, but the English type of formal garden involving avenues, water, walled enclosures and glimpses

out to the surrounding countryside is really a marriage between the two schools. Late 17th-century gardens are represented here by **Westbury Court** (70, G) which is both small and contained, bearing little relationship to the surrounding countryside. It has been chosen because it of all gardens is most like the early 18th-century Kip engravings from the series which give us the most detailed knowledge of what these gardens were actually like, with their vistas and the endless rows of lollipop trees.

Of the larger-scale parks the best survivor is probably Hampton Court in Middlesex and, moving into the beginning of the 18th century, Cirencester Park (G) which is the Bridgeman- or Kent-type survivor with a combination of large-scale avenues with a more naturalistic treatment of dense planting in between the vistas. Of the smaller-scale Kent designs the very intimate gardens of Chiswick House, London – now in the process of an extensive programme of restoration to bring them back closer to their original appearance – are the best. The survival of these formal landscapes was very quickly jeopardised by the beginnings of the more informal treatment of landscape, first the 'Arcadian' sort represented here by the most influential of all, that at **Stourhead** (69, W) and then the 'Capability' Brown type of landscape with all formality gone and the 'natural' but very carefully edited countryside lapping up to the very windows of the houses. These developments coincided with the maturing of the trees planted in the earlier formal designs so that their original appearance was now gone, and the trees were ready for incorporating into the new schemes. Formal gardening too was very much more labour intensive and costly than the 'natural' style and the result was that almost all the earlier landscapes were redesigned, leaving a few fragments, earth- and waterworks and the Kip

Arcadia at Stourhead, with the temples of Flora and Apollo. BTA/ETB

71

engravings to demonstrate just how all-pervasive they had been.

The Stourhead type of 'Arcadian' landscape was inspired by ideas culled mainly from paintings and very expensive to achieve, involving the building of grottos, temples, and dams. Capability Brown's designs were also costly, being on a larger scale and often demanding big dams and enormous numbers of trees, but maintenance was cheaper. These 'landscape gardens' (the term originated at this period) are so suited to the English temperament that they have successfully resisted all later styles and have survived in large numbers. **Bowood** (65, W) is one of the finest examples. In the 18th century grass had to be scythed and grazing was the only practical way of managing large areas. It was sometimes the case too that the landowner insisted on invisible servicing for his grounds with all workers gone by 9 or 10 am so that the eye should not be offended. This was one reason why the ha-ha fence was invented, allowing cattle to graze as near to the house as was acceptable and yet giving the impression of tailored greensward stretching away to the lake. The other particular characteristic of these landscape gardens was the muted colours of leaf and water, with very few flowers, and it is this effect that has often been marred by massed planting of rhododendrons and other flowering shrubs by the Victorians; the strident colours at Stourhead leading eventually to the National Trust removing many of the ones around the Pantheon where they were particularly ostentatious. Public opinion, however, tends to favour the rhododendrons, Stourhead for example receiving its greatest number of visitors in the flowering season, so the complete restoration of the original intention is very difficult. Rhododendrons were not available in the 1740s – if they had been they may have been used at Stourhead, but then they would have had to have featured in the paintings of Claude and Poussin as well. Luckily a genuine 18th-century effect is still possible at other seasons, and autumn and winter are also very rewarding at Stourhead when the trees can be seen at their best and there are

not so many visitors.

At the end of the 18th century the less artificially 'natural' school of landscape took over under the principal guidance of Humphry Repton. There were two main themes. Firstly the further development of Capability Brown's ideas through the clumping of trees in massed banks of varied foliage with contrasting colours and textures. Bristol (A) has a particularly fine park in this manner at Ashton Court with large areas of carefully sculptured parkland around a fine house, with hanging woods behind along the combes and ridges. Alternatively there was the 'picturesque' school of romantic landscape improvement which arose through the teachings of William Gilpin, the poetry of Wordsworth and the painting of the English landscape school bred in Italy and led by Richard Wilson and John Robert Cozens. This involved waterfalls, dashing streams, beetling cliffs, dark overhanging woods and, if possible, a bandit or two, or at least the expectation that they might be encountered around the next corner. **Blaise Castle Estate** (64, A), now a public park in Bristol, is one of the best of these with the natural rocky outlines of the park exaggerated by running the principal drives up and down steep hairpin bends, beneath overhangs and past robbers' dens and hermits' caves. Some of this romance rubbed off later in the century on the large cemeteries laid out by private companies adjacent to the great cities. The 'Elysian Fields' of Greek mythology was the principal idea behind them, but the presence of thousands of memorials and mausolea could only bring a degree of Gothic horror as well, and the two ideas mingled in such places as exemplified here by **Arnos Vale** (63, A) on the east side of Bristol.

The mid-19th century saw the increased use of gardens as places for the education, edification and recreation of the public. The first botanic garden was opened at Oxford University in 1621 and was always available to the public, and the Royal Botanic Garden at Kew in Surrey dates from 1759. During Victoria's reign botanic gardens, arboreta and public parks generally proliferated as wide exploration brought

many new species into the country, particularly from America, China and the Himalayas, and the reign of the rhododendron, the Wellingtonia, and the monkey puzzle began. **Westonbirt Arboretum** (71, G) is the finest of all the private tree collections, though Batsford (G) is also very good; while the **Royal Victoria Park** in Bath (68, A) is the very first of all municipal public parks and was soon copied by every town of any pride, and the botanic garden there is the only one to be founded (and is still maintained by) a municipality. The only other botanic garden in the area is at Bristol University, and is open to the public during the week, but not at weekends.

The far greater rigidity of Victorian life after the excesses of the Regency period was quickly reflected in gardening terms by the return to formality and, through the influence of George Kennedy and William Nesfield, the re-introduction of 17th-century style parterres and balustraded terraces to the main garden fronts of the great country houses. These intricate designs, often incorporating family mottos and the like, were made up of shaped beds filled with brightly coloured annuals, outlined by gravel and framed in grass neatly cut with the new lawnmowers. The effect was dazzling, literally a carpet of flowers, but was enormously labour intensive and could only be undertaken in an age when manpower was cheap and available. Where they survive, these schemes are little more than shadows of their former glory unless very special circumstances prevail such as a resident gardening school. A closely related form was the Italian garden filled with pergolas and statues arranged with geometric formality, and these survive at both Bowood and Westonbirt, but again in simplified form.

Reaction soon followed, particularly because this form of gardening was so completely outside the scope of any but those with the largest resources. The Victorian period saw an enormous interest in gardening grow throughout society encouraged by such magazines as *Gardener's Chronicle*. The ordinary gardener wanted something more attainable than the grand gardens of the

design excellence – with mixed colours and textures provided by plants suited to their environment, which propagated easily, needed little maintainance, and gave changing displays. These ideas of massed planting, placed within a strong architectural framework, are the basis of the successful partnership between Gertrude Jekyll and Edwin Lutyens, and are very successfully displayed in the garden at **Hestercombe** (66, S). The making of such architectural gardens is immensely expensive but each one has ideas that the visitor can apply to his own garden. The public's relationship to Lawrence Johnson's **Hidcote** (67, G) is very closely based on this, for his wonderful garden is divided up into small 'rooms', any of which might give ideas to the visitor or be related to his own garden. Hidcote still appears to be the most influential garden of the 20th century.

63

Arnos Vale Cemetery, Bristol, Avon
1837–1838

ST 607716. On Bath Rd (A4), 2 miles E of Bristol city centre

[C]

Arcadian landscapes are not confined to the pleasure grounds of country houses; in the early 19th century they were adopted as the appropriate style for the new and very large-scale cemeteries made necessary by the closure of the graveyards of city centre parish churches. These new cemeteries were set up by private companies and designed to the highest standards to attract a respectable clientele, and were inspired by the classical paintings of Nicholas Poussin, such as *The Ashes of Phocion* in the Walker Art Gallery, Liverpool. An Arcadian landscape set with classical temples, urns and sarcophagi was the ideal, and in Bristol it was supplied by Charles Underwood, a local Greek Revival architect. The entrance lodges mark it as both solemn and classically inspired, with two tiny Doric temples in Bathstone ashlar, sturdy cast-iron railings and a gate on

Arnos Vale Cemetery, a tomb for a rajah, Rammohun Roy Bahadoor. MR

rich. With this began the school of English gardening which still prevails today. Gardening as a hobby rather than a necessity was first encouraged in 1822 by J C Loudon's *Encyclopaedia of Gardening*, a publication which brought shrubberies, ferneries, and rockeries into fashion. His *The Suburban Gardener and Villa Companion* was aimed at a completely new kind of gardener, who was given further help by

Edward Kemp in 1850 in his straightforward *How to Lay out a Garden*. However, it was not until William Robinson's *The Wild Garden* (1878) and *The English Flower Garden* (1883) were published that gardeners suddenly realised they could cultivate their own gardens without elaborate teaching and that English cottage gardens, instead of being dull and unsophisticated, could be the epitome of

rollers. Within are two mortuary chapels – the Church of England one is Corinthian, the Nonconformist (no longer used) is Ionic – in a landscaped setting now entirely filled by memorials of all shapes, sizes and elaboration. Particularly notable are a large obelisk of 1866, and another to the American Consul of 1857, both by Tyley, a local mason, but the real gem is the 1843 memorial to Rajah Rammohun Roy Bahadoor in an Indian romantic manner. The further you explore from the gates and chapels, the more neglected and rather creepy the cemetery becomes. With the implementation of the 1854 Metropolitan Cemeteries Act, cemetery architecture became almost universally Gothic in style and graves were arranged in strict lines, but for twenty-five years Arcadia reigned supreme at sites such as Arnos Vale.

64
Blaise Castle Estate, Avon
1762–1810

ST 559783. At Henbury, 3 miles N of Bristol city centre

[C]

The layout of Blaise Castle grounds involves two important types of landscape design, the 'sublime' and the 'picturesque'. Originally there was a late 17th-century formal layout based on the now demolished Great House, but this

Blaise Castle. MR

74

Bowood, the view from the terrace over the south lawn and the lake. CL

was largely supplanted by Thomas Farr, a West Indian sugar merchant who purchased the estate in 1762. He proceeded to lay out a pleasure ground based on Castle Hill, an Iron Age hillfort. Blaise Castle was built within its ramparts, an important early Gothic Revival folly designed by Robert Mylne and immortalised by Jane Austen in *Northanger Abbey*:

> "Blaize Castle!" cried Catherine. "What is that?"
> "The finest place in England – worth going fifty miles at any time to see."
> "What, is it really a castle, an old castle?"
> "The oldest in the Kingdom."
> "But is it like what one reads of?"
> "Exactly – the very same."
> "But now really – are there towers and long galleries?"
> "By dozens."
> "Then I should like to see it."
> (*Northanger Abbey*, chapter 10)

John Scandrett Harford, a prominent Bristol banker, purchased the estate in 1789 and built the main house, designed by William Paty in 1799. He employed Humphry Repton to redesign the park in the 'picturesque' manner, and Blaise is the best surviving example of his work in this area. The walks, and the Robbers' Cave, from the earlier period were incorporated in a much enlarged

landscape. All the features recommended in the surviving Red Book still remain: the carriage drive, the castellated lodge and the Woodman's cottage. Indeed the whole landscape and character as originally planned can still be seen. Some tree-thinning in recent years has opened up views again, particularly the vista up from the house to the restored castle. The park has a very good series of buildings from both periods including an outstanding dairy house (1804) by John Nash, and a 'root house' (constructed of tree roots and thatched), while Blaise Hamlet (72, A) is nearby.

65
Bowood, Wiltshire
18th–19th century

ST 975699. Between Chippenham and Calne on S side of A4

[A]

The name most commonly associated with the English landscape garden in the 18th century is Lancelot 'Capability' Brown (indeed it was he who invented the term) and the park at Bowood is one of his best surviving and most satisfactory creations. The only unhappy element is that there is no longer a large house to be set off by the park and to provide a focus; it was mostly pulled down in 1955. What remains is fine enough, particularly the Robert Adam south front of 1768, once an orangery and now a picture gallery, but this is long and low and does not have sufficient mass to dominate the ridge and the lake as the house once did. Brown created the immense sweep of turf, now said to be the largest lawn in England, down to a sinuous lake with woodland mounting to the rim of the view beyond. The result is a carefully ordered and seemingly natural landscape where nothing jars; a vale of tranquillity, with little colour beyond grass, foliage and water. The rhododendrons, of which there is a magnificent collection, are well away from all this, hidden in the woods, the Victorian owners having shown an unusual degree of sophistication in preserving intact the 18th-century landscape near the house. The lake, with its dam cunningly hidden in trees, looks most natural, enhanced by the Brownian temple beyond, which was only moved there in 1864. Other outstanding features are the rockwork grottoes and cascade (entry 50), the pinetum begun in 1848, and the terraces and Italian

garden by George Kennedy (1851) which are very good examples of the genre. The Brown landscape originally extended much further with clumps, woods and rides, but although much of this survives, the pastures between have gone to the plough. The rhododendron woods which contain the Adam mausoleum of 1761–5 are entered separately and are open only during the flowering season.

66

Hestercombe, Somerset
1904

ST 240288. 3 miles N of Taunton, on minor road between Kingston St Mary and West Monkton

[A]

The reaction against the use of brightly coloured annuals in formal patterns as the centrepieces of the larger Victorian gardens began with the publication of William Robinson's *The English Flower Garden* in 1883. The move was now towards informal massing of flowering plants. Cottage garden flowers were the

new vogue, arranged in relation to architectural features rather than the formal geometry of the beds themselves. There appeared a more subtle approach to form and texture in borders and beds as well as in the design of walls, paths and other built elements. The partnership of Gertrude Jekyll, the artist plantswoman and most influential author, and Edwin Lutyens the master architect produced this garden, certainly one of their best. Commissioned in 1904 by Viscount Portman as a modern garden within the remains of Coplestone Bamfyld's late 18th-century park it proved an inspiration to Lutyens who designed a wonderful architectural layout enhanced by Miss Jekyll's planting. The one sad aspect is the house itself, a dull Victorian reconstruction of the 18th-century house, for a garden without a good house does not seem complete.

The main area of the garden stands immediately below the south front on ground which fell away towards the Vale of Taunton. Lutyens created raised terraces surrounding a formal 'plat', the one on the south surmounted by a long pergola. These provide wonderful vistas and contrasting views of the formal garden within and the 'natural' countryside beyond. This arrangement distracts attention from the facade of the house. To the east of the house is Lutyens's Italianate Orangery and the little Dutch garden – built as a raised terrace on top of an old rubbish dump – which look out over a fine lawn. The area to the south and that to the east are cleverly articulated by the Rotunda. The formal use of water is an important element in this garden, as testified by the two circular pools set in alcoves with mask water spouts, the long rills with looped stone detail and the sunken bathing tanks – used by Lutyens elsewhere. The rough split stone, quarried behind the house, contrasts pleasingly with the Ham stone dressings, and all architectural detailing is superb. As Somerset County Council's restoration continues towards completion, and the new planting matures, it will stand as a fitting memorial to this great gardening partnership.

Hestercombe from the north-west, with the west rill and 'plat'. RCHME

Hidcote topiary garden. BTA/ETB

67

Hidcote, Gloucestershire
1904–1948

SP 176429. 3 miles N of Chipping Campden, on minor road off B4081

[A] NT

The area is fortunate to contain what must be the most influential of all 20th-century gardens, the Hidcote of Lawrence Johnson. In 1904 he took an unpromisingly barren and windswept site and spent over forty years transforming it into a garden which now finds response in every gardener, however large or small one's plot and ambitions. Working on from the principles of Gertrude Jekyll (see Hestercombe, 66, S), Johnson created a series of interconnected contrasting rooms within the necessary shelter planting – some formal, some more like cottage gardens, and some woodland. The open wold is not an easy site but it does provide a good growing ground for beeches, wonderful views and a varied skyscape, and these have been incorporated into a cohesive whole which brings interest round every corner, encouraging the desire to explore further and look everywhere. This is the same kind of conception as at Stourhead (69, W) but on quite a different scale and with different philosophical ideas behind it. It is intimate, each space is small and the whole is only 10 acres, yet the surrounding landscape is used in the cleverest way making the whole as large in concept as you like. There are views out in all directions but really no views in, and so it remains a private world, if that can be possible in one of the National Trust's most visited gardens. Lawrence Johnson's French connections are evident in the strong geometrical and architectural qualities of Hidcote but they are softened by the English character of the planting, and by the low profiles of the actual buildings. There is no Lutyens here to give the plants a vigorous foil; the walls are mostly alive and green rather than brick or stone. It must not be imagined that this is purely a garden for the designer and the architect – Hidcote has an important plant collection as well, shown by the number of varieties which bear its name.

68

Royal Victoria Park and Botanic Garden, Bath, Avon
1830 and 1888

ST 740655. 1 mile W of city centre

[C]

Although modest in size and design, the Royal Victoria Park has a unique position in the history of municipal gardening. It was the country's first proper public park and, later in the 19th century, no English city was to consider itself complete without one. The Botanic Garden, established in one corner in 1888, was the first and indeed the only such garden in the country to be founded and maintained by the local corporation. The park was laid out on land known as the Lower Common which belonged to the Bath Corporation. There were no public gardens in the city, only subscription pleasure gardens like Sydney Gardens, and private communal gardens like those in Queen Square.

Edward Davis's design was inspired by the fashionable royal parks in London with a carriage drive around the perimeter, cross walks, a small lake and a good number of specimen trees. The park was opened by the eleven-year-old Princess Victoria and, seven years later, the obelisk, designed by G P Manners, was erected to commemorate her majority a few months before her accession to the throne. The 150 years since has seen the park develop and the trees grow and, for its size, it must be one of the most well-used parks in the

Royal Victoria Park and Botanic Garden: the advent of spring. MR

country, both in general and with special events like the annual flower and horse shows and the Bank Holiday fairs.

The corporation quickly decided it wanted an educational garden as well and an area was set aside for a botanic garden in 1840, but it was not until 1887 when a gift of 2,000 plants from a Mr Broome of Batheaston, coinciding with the Queen's Golden Jubilee, led to the foundation of the pretty Botanic Garden of today. In its centenary year of 1988 it expanded into the Great Dell to the north and now includes a pinetum. The original intention was for it to be a demonstration limestone garden. This remains an important role, but since the foundation of the Botany Department at Bath University it has also fulfilled the traditional botanic garden function of providing specimens for study. Unfortunately no early plans survive, and it is not known when the arrangement of features like the pool and the herbaceous border was first introduced. The garden's only building was originally the Bath pavilion at the British Empire Exhibition at Wembley in 1926.

Stourhead, the bridge and the Pantheon. EH

69

Stourhead, Wiltshire
1722–1838

ST 775340. 3 miles NW of Mere, off B3092

[A] NT

Stourhead is both the originator and the finest example of the English 'idyllic' or 'Arcadian' landscape. In the 18th century an essential component of an aristocratic education was the continental 'Grand Tour' and it was through this that the ideas of Arcadia originated, based on the landscape of the Campagna around Rome, and the paintings of Nicholas and Gaspard Poussin and the much collected Claude Lorraine. It was a romanticised classicism with quite an element of voyeurism. At Stourhead you actually find yourself in a picture by Claude with a view of the temple glimpsed through the trees in the distance, but here at last you can arrive at it, see inside it and

then move on to other delights hidden round other corners. It is a progression of visual adventures with the expectation of surprising the faun and the shepherdess, or even Diana herself. It is difficult to see it as a private world, for its fame has always brought throngs of visitors to its relatively small compass, but the thick underplanting of flowering shrubs among the magnificent mature trees means that large numbers of visitors can be hidden with only their cries and laughter coming across the lake as if they might yet be nymphs and satyrs. The original layout (1722–87) was by Henry Hoare and with extensive additional planting by his nephew Richard Colt Hoare between 1787 and 1838. To appreciate the proper 18th-century contrasts of foliage and bark colours, and the movement and reflection of leaf and water, the rhododendron flowering season is better avoided, but it is wonderful at any season.

It is not just the planting which is stunning – three of the buildings are outstandingly fine, the Pantheon (1753), the Temple of Apollo (1757) and the Grotto (1748) all designed by Henry Flitcroft; and there are many more.

70

Westbury Court Garden, Gloucestershire
1696–1705 and c.1715–1720

SO 718138. At Westbury-on-Severn, 10 miles W of Gloucester on A48

[A] NT

The fashion for Dutch gardens which overtook the English following the arrival of William of Orange in 1689 is now represented by very little on the ground, though the detailed early 18th-century bird's eye drawings by Kip show just how widespread it was. Formal gardens of the late 17th and early 18th centuries have dual parentage, Dutch and French. The French style is based on the wider ambitions of Le Nôtre with avenues stretching into the landscape. The Dutch is more intimate with the emphasis on enclosure, usefulness (the production of fruit, vegetables and flowers for cutting) and particularly on use of water as a feature, so easily come by in Holland. Long vistas were provided by canals and accentuated by trees in rigid lines and the visual stops of tall summerhouses from which both the

Westbury Court Garden, the T-canal with the summerhouse to the right. MR

garden design and the surrounding countryside could be admired. The only English garden which still clearly demonstrates these themes is the one at Westbury, which has survived the demolition of three parent houses, the removal of the family for a long period, and eventual wholesale dereliction. Between 1967 and 1978 the local authorities and the National Trust reconstructed it, using the detailed account books of the original owner Maynard Colchester, found in the Gloucester Record Office. These have confirmed many of the details of the Kip drawing of c.1707, some of which had previously been thought fanciful, and now the garden is once again approaching its original appearance. The reconstruction of the summerhouse has not been entirely successful, as the brickwork is incorrect, but otherwise the garden is a triumph. The surviving features appear to be of two phases of work: the Long Canal, summerhouse and road wall of 1696–1705 by Maynard Colchester I and the eastward extension with the T-canal, the walled garden and the gazebo of c.1715 by his nephew Maynard Colchester II. The only part of the restoration which is not authentic is

the incorporation of part of a parterre within the garden. This was really some distance away in front of the now-demolished 17th-century house, and dates from an earlier period, although the Kip drawing shows it still to have been in existence when the Dutch garden was laid out. Only at Dyrham Park (A) does a similar garden survive and there it is the barest of bones, while at Westbury we once again have the appearance of the real thing.

71

Westonbirt Arboretum, Gloucestershire
19th century

ST 848898. 3 miles SW of Tetbury on W side of A433

[A]

The planting of this famous arboretum was begun by R S Holford in 1829 well before the present house (entry 60) was built, and is thus related to the previous house on the site which stood in an 18th-century park that still largely survives. The high road (now the A433) divided the arboretum from the park,

but this handicap was ignored. The landscape vaults the road and the eye is drawn into the arboretum along early 18th-century style avenues radiating from within the park itself. These avenues were set out with the finest and largest of the North American trees which were introduced in the 1840s and 50s and are now magnificently mature: Douglas Firs and Wellingtonias in particular, but also many other species. This, of course, gives an effect completely unknown in the 18th century when avenues of beech or lime would have been in order.

Between the avenues the trees are arranged around glades with smaller specimen trees and shrubs, notably the Japanese maples which bring the autumn visitors, but the layout has always kept the large trees in mind. The best and biggest examples can be seen from base to tip, and there is really nowhere else where so many superb foreign trees can be admired in such a way. Far Eastern trees were the particular interest of Sir George Holford from 1870 onwards, but every continent is represented and Sir George extended the planted area, planting 'The Silk Wood' to the south and west. This is a more informal layout with winding drives and larger glades where full-sized examples of British and European trees of all kinds can be enjoyed as well as species from other continents. The Forestry Commission, owners since 1956, have worked to increase the numbers of visitors with the result that, on a fine October afternoon, the main walks are uncomfortably crowded – but do not be deterred, for even then it is possible to find a corner of one's own.

Westonbirt Arboretum.
FORESTRY COMMISSION

7

Society and the Law: Estate Villages and Institutions

One aspect of English life which is particularly well represented through its surviving buildings is the awakening social conscience of the English people. This was demonstrated through a new sense of responsibility amongst the establishment for those who worked for them or lived on their land, and the evangelising of ideas of fair treatment amongst those who saw themselves at the bottom of the pile, but now began to sense that the Industrial Revolution was giving them a new importance – a strength and influence with which to negotiate with their masters towards their own betterment. These ideas were not entirely new in the 18th and 19th centuries, but there are few physical remains to remind us of earlier periods.

Only a cataclysm could really upset the English establishment, but this happened in the Middle Ages with the Black Death, when, in 1348 and the years following, the working population was cut by between 30 and 50 per cent and the scarcity of labour in agriculture and in the woollen and other industries was exacerbated by the increased demands on manpower made by the wars in France, though the lull following the crushing victory at Poitiers in 1356 did ease that pressure.

This section is primarily concerned with the period of social upheaval between 1750 and 1850, and the first tentative improvements in the lot of the common people, together with some of the ways in which the establishment strengthened itself against the challenge. It is divided into two parts: new villages or groups of workers' houses, and institutional buildings, selected from the many kinds built in response to the legislation of the period and the new philanthropy, when both education and the law began to move towards less repressive practices, though these improvements were strictly relative.

In the case of the villages, and in working-class housing generally, there was a real improvement, but it was improvement from appalling and unimaginable rural slums to a condition of tolerable discomfort. Villages were founded for many reasons in the period but they were more often the work of landowners wishing to improve their own surroundings and moral standing rather than the living conditions of their tenants. **Milton Abbas** (76, D) is a village famed for its pretty appearance, but if you look at the lie of the land you realise just how carefully the houses have been sited in the long wooded combe so as to be completely hidden from the landowner's view except when it pleases him to see them. The sweeping views of idyllic Capability Brown parkland were not for the tenants, who instead found themselves, then as now, to be objects of interest to visitors, who could look without having to share in the rigours of their lives. I wonder how many of the people who live there now look upon themselves as figures in an animated painting of rural life, for that is what they were intended to be?

Blaise Hamlet (72, A) is basically similar, an exercise in the 'picturesque', where appearance comes a long way ahead of considerations of comfort and convenience, though the cottages are not quite as small and poky as they appear to be. Sandy Lane near Chippenham (W) is another, even more successfully 'picturesque' village in the area which would have been included in this selection if there had been more to say about it. Little seems to be known of its provenance or even its date; Gillian Darley's *Villages of Vision* (1975) passes it by with a gazetteer entry: 'Sandy Lane, stone and thatch model village'. Rows of extremely picturesque thatched cottages line the road between pub and church, and even the church is thatched, though that is a piece of early 20th-century whimsy. Some of the cottages appear to have origins in the 17th century (but the

Crowdown Lodge, Grittleton, with its signalling tower. MR

whole must be an early 19th-century conception) and they look wonderfully effective against the background of cottage gardens and woodland. A rather different effect was achieved at nearby Erlestoke (W) where cottages built around 1800 were decorated with carved timbers cannibalised from ancient buildings. Such 'olde worlde' contrivance was most uncommon at this time and usually associated with the last, not the first, years of the 19th century.

There are few industrial estate villages in the area but **Swindon Railway Village** (80, W) is a particularly good example, and can only really be compared locally with the Somerset town of Street which was built in the 1880s on behalf of the Clark family, whose shoe factory is still there. Here the individual quality of the building is not high, but the overall effect is both consistent and curious, with knobbly stone walls and steeply gabled roofs.

The public schools saw much building in the 19th century to cater for an expanding middle class, and to provide the new kind of training, not based solely on classical studies, advocated by Dr Thomas Arnold of Rugby School and needed by the professions and the Civil Service. **Cheltenham College** (73, G) was a new foundation set up for just this purpose.

The best of the 18th-century hospitals is probably the Royal Mineral Water Hospital in Bath, a fine design by John Wood the elder dating from 1738–42 and certainly worth looking at on a visit to the city. The first Principal was Dr Oliver of Bath Oliver biscuits fame. The county infirmaries in both Taunton (S) and Salisbury (W) have some surviving 18th-century buildings, but sadly the particularly good one at Gloucester was demolished some years ago. Mendip Hospital, Wells (S) is a fine example of a County Lunatic Asylum (Scott and Moffat, 1838) while Brockworth Hospital (1888) outside Gloucester was the first example of the echelon plan which was subsequently adopted for all such asylums.

In this area the buildings of the law – the workhouse, court and the prisons – cannot be bettered as surviving examples of their type and period. The workhouse system set up by the 1834 Poor Law Amendment Act was an improvement on the haphazard methods of poverty relief which prevailed before, but the system was open to great abuse, as Dickens describes so memorably in *Oliver Twist*, published in 1838 just as **Williton Union Workhouse** (83, S) was being completed. This workhouse has been preserved, like so many others, by becoming the local hospital when the system was wound up by the Local Government Act in 1929. Dorchester Crown Court has been preserved as a memorial to the Tolpuddle Martyrs; and prisons became police stations and thus survived the period before their historical value was realised. Freed from

the stigma of their original uses they can now be visited with enjoyment, and seen as part of a reformed system, now thankfully improved again. The architecture of these buildings demonstrates their purpose very clearly and, however they may be reused, their original function will never be fully obscured. They are not building types commonly brought to the attention of tourists and yet there is much to be learnt from them.

A standing army made an increasing impact on English life during the 18th century as the continental mercenaries were paid off to be replaced by the 'redcoats', first professionalised by the Duke of Marlborough, strengthened because of the invasion from Scotland in

The women's prison of 1844 at Northleach House of Correction. MR

1745 and then boosted by the Scots themselves who, caught between starvation following eviction and the army, chose the latter. These troops were maintained not only for fighting foreign enemies but to maintain law and order at home in times of civil unrest. There are no particularly good examples of depots, barracks and other military buildings in the area although the cavalry barracks at Tidworth Camp (*c*.1900), partly in Wiltshire and partly in Hampshire, are certainly interesting, though security prevents more than a distant view and lingering is not encouraged.

72

Blaise Hamlet, Avon
1809–1813

ST 560788. At Henbury, 3 miles N of Bristol city centre
[D] NT

The nine cottages which make up Blaise Hamlet have a lot to answer for. It is indeed right for the National Trust to own them, for these whimsical designs are responsible for the character of much of the merchandise in their shops, from thatched teapots to Christmas cards. Is this really what rural England in the early 19th century was all about? Certainly not. Designed by Nash and Repton, these were dwellings intended for the comfort of retired employees of the Harford estate (see Blaise Castle Estate, 64, A) and were carefully designed for a reasonable standard of accommodation, but with the interior planning very subordinated to the exterior appearance: 'The Coppers and

Swindon Railway Village: glimpse of a back lane with outhouses in Church Place. MR

Ovens can have but little spaces allowed for them. The gardner [*sic*] must therefore enquire and find out the smallest sized coppers and ovens that will be sufficient for the sort of people who will live in the Cottages and let them be built accordingly' (G Repton, 1811).

There is tremendous variety of texture and form using a number of different building materials, but the impression somehow is that they are all thatched (in fact only three are), that all have diamond leaded lights (only three do) and that they all have tall round chimneys (these occur on only two). Nash did not design them especially for this site; all the cottage designs had been built elsewhere. To collect them all together was, however, a new and daring idea, an early theme park in which the gnarled inhabitants were part of the attraction. Perfectly picturesque, the cottages are carefully disposed around an uneven green, with all doors facing in different directions, supposedly to discourage nosiness among the residents. They are undeniably charming, and important architecturally, but would you like to live there? The central sundial was erected in 1815 and records Harford's son's belief in their value.

73

Cheltenham College, Gloucestershire
1823–1864

SO 948214. On Bath Rd ½ mile S of town centre
[C] and **[D]**

Cheltenham College (Boys) is one of the most satisfactory groups of buildings in the town, a mixture of quality and quirkiness in several different styles and by a number of architects. Founded as a result of Cheltenham's established reputation for 'curry and colonels' it was a 'proprietary' college set up by a group of shareholders with the purpose of training boys for the Indian Army and Civil Service, but had little endowment and to begin with had to be content with fairly cheap buildings. The original block, on Bath Road, is in the Tudor Gothic style with a central tower flanked by the 'Big Classical' and 'Big Modern' schoolrooms, now theatre and library. It is an attractive building by the Bath architect James Wilson and must have inspired the same architect's commission for the more complicated Kingswood School on Lansdown, Bath, which dates from 1851.

Cheltenham College, the original block on Bath Road. MR

The idea of large, lofty schoolrooms was still current in the early Victorian period, having originated in the medieval schools like Eton and Winchester, but was already being superseded by a classical style of school design with smaller schoolrooms and lower ceilings, as at Haileybury. The college quickly expanded with additional building in the Perpendicular style. The old chapel (now the dining hall) was designed by D J Humphries and built in the 1850s, and the Junior School by John Middleton a decade later. The school has two other remarkable buildings. The Gymnasium (1864) by F H Lockwood flanks the cricket ground and is a wonderful long range in yellow brick with contrasting brickwork decoration and ironwork supporting the balconies. Its design is supposed to bear a relationship to the Bombay Telegraph Office (W Paris, 1871–4), and the balconies and turrets certainly give a feeling of the Raj, making it one of the most charming of those Victorian institutional buildings which are both ugly and attractive.

In complete contrast is Thirlestaine House (J R Scott, 1823), the large and fine Greek villa to the right of the college in Bath Road, which became a part of the college in 1945. Apparently designed by the owner, its Ionic portico

Blaise Hamlet, the sundial with Circular Cottage (left) and Vine Cottage (right). MR

clearly owes something to Downing College, Cambridge, and predates the Pittville Pump Room (45, G). The wings were added by Lord Northwick in 1840 and 1845 to house his pictures.

74

Dorchester Shire Hall and Crown Court, Dorset
1797

SY 690907. On High St in town centre

[A]

Dorchester has enjoyed rather an uncertain status as the county town of Dorset. Founded by the Romans as a deliberate demonstration of colonial power after the fall of Maiden Castle (17, D), it never developed significantly in size, had no cathedral and lacked style as an administrative and social centre. At

the end of the 18th century however, some civic development took place: a county gaol designed by William Blackburn was built in 1791 (see also Northleach House of Correction, 87, G), a new town hall in 1792 (now replaced by Benjamin Ferrey's building of 1847–8), and the Shire Hall and Crown Court, in one building (by Thomas Hardwick) in 1797.

The building has a plain but handsome Portland stone front incorporating a particularly good contemporary plaque giving the mileage to Hyde Park Corner, and makes a fine contribution to the street, but it is the interior which is more important. In the Crown Court the arrangement and fittings are largely original: the judge's chair, benches, witness box, dock, and galleries carried on Roman Doric columns are all consistent in design and have been preserved by the owners (since 1956, the Trades Union Congress)

as a permanent memorial to the most famous occupants of the dock, the six Tolpuddle Martyrs (see entry 82) condemned in 1834 to the penal settlements of New South Wales on a trumped-up charge. No evidence was produced to show that they were other than honest sober men who had neither gone on strike nor demanded an increase in pay.

The Court is highly evocative of the period and of the awful majesty of the law in those days when you could be imprisoned for stealing a handkerchief, hung for stealing a horse and transported for seven years for taking an oath of mutual support. The new Shire Hall is immediately behind and is as characteristic of the 1930s as the old one is of the 1790s, though curiously enough the planning of the central core and radiating wings continues to owe something to the design of 19th-century prisons and workhouses.

Dorchester Shire Hall, the courtroom where the Tolpuddle Martyrs trial was held in 1834. RCHME

75

Grittleton, Wiltshire
1835–1856

ST 880860. Just N of M4 between junctions 17 and 18, NW of Chippenham

[D]

Grittleton is the result of the work of two men: the mid 19th-century landowner Joseph Neeld of Grittleton House rebuilt almost everything between 1835 and his death in 1856; and the estate's architectural character comes from the pen of architect James Thompson. It was not all built anew, for many older houses were altered and added to, producing a mid 19th-century estate village in a consistent Tudor Gothic style punctuated here and there by some quirks and oddities. Joseph Neeld was an improving landlord anxious to give his employees a better environment and living standards and, at the same time, demonstrate his own virtue in the eyes of God and England. The estate church built at Leigh Delamere in 1846 sets the tone – non-correct Gothic in style and apparently a total rebuild, though Thompson described it as 'restoration'. This marks a stage in the Gothic revival when decoration could be reasonably correct but the form of the building not at all so. Nearby there are contemporary almshouses and a rectory.

In Grittleton itself there is Grittleton House and its stables, both by Thompson. In the 1850s, the house was

Grittleton, houses in the main street. MR

altered in Jacobean style by Henry Clutton and more estate housing was built. There are several farms of architectural quality and two estate lodges, Fosse Lodge in Alderton Road and Crowdown at East Foscote, both crowned by tall and teetering towers, variously supposed to be observation towers for following the local hunt or for telegraphic signalling.

Another hamlet, Sevington, has the estate school and schoolhouse where the original decoration and furnishing of the schoolroom still survives. From the date of opening in April 1849 to closure in 1913, this school had the same teacher.

Many estate villages were built in this period but few as successfully as Grittleton.

76

Milton Abbas, Dorset
1780–1786

ST 806017. N of A354, 6 miles SW of Blandford Forum

[D]

In the 1760s Sir William Chambers was employed by Lord Dorchester to build a new country house beside the surviving church of Milton Abbey. John Vardy had already begun a Gothic design. This was demolished and Chambers began again, but in a very similar style. Once the house was completed he turned his attention to the landscape around it. Capability Brown provided designs for new Arcadian surroundings, but one problem remained: the ancient market town of Milton Abbey clustered around the church as it had done since the Middle Ages, and did not fit into the picture at all. One broken-down cottage a short distance from the house might be agreeable, but a whole town was not to be thought of. Thus arose the present village of Milton Abbas, sometimes cited as an early example of philanthropic planning but in reality a device to rid a wealthy and powerful landowner of an inconvenient blemish on his otherwise perfectly conceived 18th-century landscape. This was not an uncommon occurrence during this period, and on this occasion gave rise to something

Milton Abbas, cob-and-thatch cottages. MR

different and very attractive in itself – though not especially so for the occupants.

It has been suggested that Chambers was responsible for the overall scheme and Brown for the house designs – indeed, both Chambers and Brown produced ideas, but the records are unclear as to where the responsibility for the design ultimately lay. Certainly Chambers, who had fallen out with Lord Dorchester over travelling expenses, receded into the background, while Brown made a number of visits to the site. The village street winds up the combe lined with cottages set tactfully below the skyline and back from the road. The almshouses (1674, rebuilt 1779), re-erected from the old town, the church (1786 by James Wyatt) and the village school (mid 19th-century) – the latter two genteel gothic – are placed half-way up the street. The cottages are built of the traditional (and cheap) local materials of plastered cob walls with thatched roofs. They are apparently independent detached houses built to a very high standard of accommodation for the time, but look at them closely and you will see that those with one door in the middle are a pair of dwellings and those with a door in each gable wall are actually four dwellings, two up and two down, and must have been tiny indeed. They have been amalgamated in recent years, of course, but the original intention was not so much to give the estate worker better accommodation as to give the gentry something pleasing to the eye – an attractive street of neat houses with the inhabitants' behaviour controlled by strict covenants. The village was thus to be a tribute to Lord Dorchester's greatness rather than his concern for his tenants' welfare.

77

New Inn, Gloucester
15th and 18th century

SO 832186. In Northgate St, 150 yards N of Cross and to E of Cathedral

[C]

The area contains some of the finest medieval inns in the country, usually built by monasteries, and the New Inn is a unique survival in terms of plan. It dates from about 1450, and was built by Gloucester Abbey as an inn for the pilgrims (of lesser quality) who came to

the shrines in the Cathedral. It survives amongst the modern development of Northgate Street largely in its original form, although its external and internal character is superficially 18th century. Go through the paved carriage arch and there it is, the only medieval courtyard inn with galleries on all sides. Of course, little of what you see on the surface is really ancient, and the house style of the present owners does not enhance it, but the creeper-hung galleries with the bedrooms still opening directly off them clearly evoke coaching days even if you are not really transported fully to the 15th century. The bar on the left at the rear of the courtyard displays its ancient

origins more effectively than the rest, while the ancient structure can best be seen in the alleyway by the side entrance.

Another fine medieval inn, the George and Pilgrim at Glastonbury (S) was built for the same purpose as the New Inn. Glastonbury was another very important monastery, but lesser religious houses also had their own inns. Such a one was the George at Norton St Philip (S) which was built by the monks of nearby Hinton Charterhouse for the merchants attending the two great annual fairs, and it is of a different plan type from the New Inn, being built in the form of a great gatehouse with most of the premises fronting the street. The exterior was altered after a fire in the 16th century when the timber-framed upper floors were added, but the ground floor with its archway and two mullioned bay windows (rebuilt after traffic damage) is 15th century, and in the bars there are still carved stone fireplaces, and moulded ceiling beams which together with today's bustle and excellent Wadworth's beer still give the authentic feel of the past. The inn was used as local headquarters both by the Duke of Monmouth in 1685 and shortly after by the avenging Judge Jeffreys.

78

Northleach House of Correction, Gloucestershire
1788–1791

SP 109159. In Northleach on junction of A429 (Fosse Way) and old main road at W end of village

[A]

The late 18th century at last saw a movement towards the improvement of the atrocious prison conditions described by John Howard in *The State of Prisons in England and Wales* in 1777. The resulting outcry, from the generally largely uncaring society of the time, led to the Penitentiary Act of 1779, and the competition for the design of new prisons in which William Blackburn was successful. The new emphasis was to be on solid construction, light, air, exercise, cleanliness and the separation

New Inn, the centre courtyard looking towards the Northgate Street entrance. MR

of different classes of offenders. The planning was to be a central guard block with cells in radiating wings, the courtyards between allowing separation of the sexes and types of prisoners. The design, on the basic panopticon plan (but which was not yet fully developed by Jeremy Bentham), is basically the same as that later used in the Union Workhouses (see Williton Union Workhouse, 83, S) and in the major gaols of the early 19th century such as Dartmoor and Parkhurst. Gloucestershire was fortunate enough to elect in 1780 Sir George Onesiphorus Paul as High Sheriff and he quickly espoused gaol reform after visiting the current County Gaol. Four new buildings were put up to Blackburn's designs at Northleach, Littledean, Horsely and Lawford's Gate, Bristol. Of these four, Northleach survives in part as a result of its conversion to a police station and courthouse in the 1850s. Built at a cost of £5,111 6s. 4d., it retains the original Keeper's House and the chapel, flanked on the left by the mill house which was built for the treadwheel-driven corn mill in 1823, and on the right by the new women's cell block of 1844. The older cell blocks behind have gone, but the sense of enclosure is retained by the perimeter walls and the new display building for the Cotswold countryside collection. Some cell fittings remain, but there is more at Littledean (SO 674137) where both a block of cells and the 1874 court room survive, all surrounded by the

impressive original walls. These two buildings remain most satisfying examples of the architecture of purpose (i.e., buildings which demonstrate their use through their appearance). They are also good examples of the adaptive use of buildings, apparently very difficult to reuse, so that their physical survival is assured.

79

Snig's End, Gloucestershire
1847

SO 792290. At Staunton, 8 miles N of Gloucester on A417

[D]

The village of Staunton, encompassing Snig's End, is the best surviving example of the estates laid out by developer and architect Feargus O'Connor for the Peoples Land Company. The company was set up to give the landless poor the opportunity of owning land, and thereby escaping the miserable conditions in industrial towns (as described by Dickens and Mrs Gaskell), but in fact the allottees came from very varied backgrounds. The idea was that the company accepted investment from shareholders, land was then bought and divided up into plots. Each of these smallholdings was given a cottage and provided with livestock, then rented for a very modest sum to those successful in a lottery. Five estates were purchased and developed, of which Snig's End and

the nearby Lowbands are in our area. Snig's End covered an area of 268 acres and cost £11,000. The land was divided into 33 plots of 4 acres, 12 plots of 3 acres and 35 plots of 2 acres, the rents from which could then be used to finance other projects. Eighty-one houses, many of which survive, were built to O'Connor's standard design. A school was also built which is now the Plume of Feathers Inn. On both main approaches to the village the cottages are immediately evident, some still preserved almost complete in their original smallholding, others sadly altered. The best surviving examples can be seen in The Crescent and the lanes to the north of the main road.

But the activities of the Peoples Land Company met with disapproval in some quarters. The establishment saw this method of land acquisition as a threat to traditional patterns of ownership, and in 1848 the business of the Land Company was declared an illegal lottery.

80

Swindon Railway Village, Wiltshire
1839–1843

SU 140850. In town centre, to W of railway station

[D]

Brunel's decision to choose Swindon for the site of the locomotive and carriage works of the Great Western Railway was taken in 1839. It was the highest point of the line, and though not half-way, it marked the end of the long climb up from Bristol to the rim of the Thames valley. The works and the railway were some way to the north of the small market town and it was quickly realised that the large number of workers would need accommodation nearby. Despite the company's unwillingness, Brunel insisted on providing a planned town with workers' housing of a much higher standard than was usual at the period.

With some assistance from Matthew Digby Wyatt, Brunel designed the whole thing himself – the layout, the elevations and planning of the different classes of houses, the pubs and the

Northleach House of Correction, the Keeper's House and Chapel (centre), and treadmill house of 1823 (right). MR
(*Right*) layout plan of Snig's End (after Alice Mary Hadfield). EH

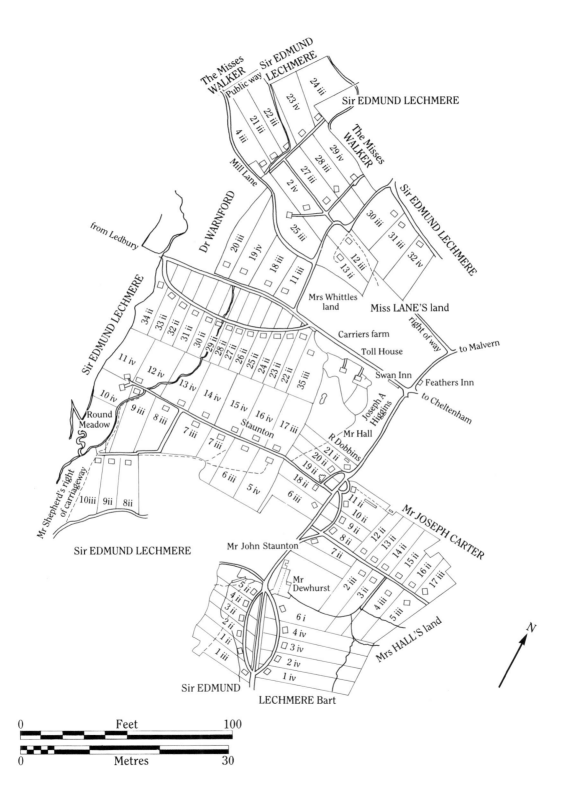

Swindon Railway Village, Exeter Street, with a foreman's house on the left. MR

Theatre Royal, the auditorium from the stage. RCHME

public buildings. The prevailing character is Tudor Gothic, a style he had used for the stations (e.g., Temple Meads, 107, A) and which he had been taught by Thomas Rickman. The cottages were a fair size with front gardens, and each was provided with a privy, wash-house and coalhouse in the backyard (the GWR museum has one furnished as a 1900 railwayman's house). Built by Messrs Rigby of London, the original 300 stone houses, ranged in terraces along wide streets, were made ready for occupation in 1843. As the village and works developed, the paternalistic company added common services – churches, dispensary, shops, market, hospital, baths, etc. – so that the railway workers' quality of life continued to be well ahead of other industrial contemporaries. All this can still be seen and although the works themselves closed in 1986 the village, after a period of decline, was rescued by a wise local authority, repaired and upgraded sensitively as council housing, and has now been sold on, with the cottages protected for the future by listing and restrictive convenants.

81
Theatre Royal, Bristol, Avon
1764–1766

ST 587726. In King St, city centre
[C]

The county of Avon is privileged to have the finest Georgian theatre in the country. The Theatre Royal, Bristol, is the oldest to have been in continuous

use in Britain, though only the auditorium survives, and that was much altered and redecorated in 1800 and again later in the 19th century. As originally designed by James Paty the Younger, it had a horseshoe auditorium with stage boxes, pit, stall boxes and circle. The stage boxes, framed by Corinthian pilasters, remain, as do the Doric columns supporting the galleries and the decorative entablature. In 1800 the roof was heightened to form a further gallery, and there was new plaster decoration, some of which remains. In 1971 the whole theatre was remodelled except for the auditorium. The new street facade is a pleasant modern design by Peter Moro, and the foyer adapts what was Coopers Hall, a Palladian building of 1743–4 by William Halfpenny with the replica ceiling of its first-floor hall hanging fairly unhappily over the modern staircase. An unfortunate victim of this rebuilding was the old stage machinery.

Its rival in Bath, built in 1804–5, also the Theatre Royal, has what Bristol does not, the exterior of a Georgian playhouse designed by an important architect, George Dance the Younger, but the interior is not quite so good. The auditorium had a serious fire in 1863 and was rebuilt in a fairly florid Victorian manner by C J Phipps, who also added the entrance in the Sawclose; but much of its Georgian character has been recovered during the recent restoration in 1980–2. A visit to both is highly recommended, especially if there is a good play on, but do be careful about the choice of seats – originally the columns were incorporated in the box divisions, but not so today!

82
Tolpuddle, Dorset

SY 790945. 7 miles E of Dorchester on A35
[D]

Forever to be associated with one of the most unjust acts of the British establishment, the pleasant but unremarkable Dorset village of Tolpuddle is still filled with memories of the 'bad old days' of 1834. Interest centres on the so-called Martyrs' Cottage, an undistinguished 18th-century building which was once the home of Thomas Standfield, one of the six martyrs, and the meeting-place where the Friendly Society of Agricultural Labourers was founded on the lines of the Grand National Trade Union and the oath of mutual support taken which led to the six being tried, condemned, and sentenced to seven years transportation to New South Wales. The crime was not the formation of the trade union but the taking of the oath. The landed establishment, having cut agricultural wages from 10s. to 7s. a week, which was below subsistence level, feared revolution and the Mutiny Act of 1797 was invoked. This Act had been passed thirty-seven years earlier to deal with trouble in the Navy following the mutinies against conditions on the ships anchored at the Nore and Spithead. There was an immediate public outcry against the evident injustice of the conviction but the martyrs had been rushed out of the country. The men were not pardoned until 1837, and returned to England in 1838, but only one, James Hammett, went back to live in Tolpuddle. His grave is in the churchyard, with a headstone by Eric Gill. The others left disillusioned for a new life in Canada. The TUC keep their memory alive with the Memorial Almshouses and library in the village. The Methodist chapel where five of the martyrs worshipped, and where one, George Loveless, was minister, also survives though now a barn and the visitor may also see its replacement chapel with the memorial archway in the main street. The Dorchester court-room in which the trial took place is also preserved (74, D).

83

Williton Union Workhouse, Somerset
1838–40

SS 083414. On A39 near Williton railway station

[D]

The Poor Law Amendment Act of 1834 revised the Elizabethan Poor Law of 1601 which required each parish to look after its own destitute. The latter measure had been principally designed to restrict vagrancy which was endemic in the period. The system was always open to abuse and in the 19th century there was pressure for change. The new Act required groups or unions of parishes each to construct a workhouse according to design conditions set out by the government. They were to be run by Boards of Trustees, the 'Guardians of the Poor', and administered by the beadle, portrayed unforgettably by Dickens in the shape of Mr Bumble. Workhouses were to be built on a variation of the panopticon principle invented by Jeremy Bentham in the

Williton Union Workhouse, the entrance and central block from the A39. MR

1790s for use in prisons. This meant that cell blocks, wards in the case of workhouses, radiated from a central higher observation block for the wardens. Bentham's design was not worked out in full until the building of the Millbank Penitentiary (1813) on the site of the Tate Gallery. The first workhouse designs were by Sampson Kempthorne, architect to the Poor Law Commission, and that at Abingdon (1836) acted as a model. This has now been very altered but many imitations survive.

G G Scott and William Moffatt were among the leading designers of workhouses in the late 1830s and a number of their buildings remain, Williton ranking among the best and most complete of these. It accommodated the destitute of the parishes in the Williton Union and is of medium size. The T-shaped wings project from a central four-storey block for the wardens. Facing the street there is a handsome entrance archway with flanking public and visiting rooms. The subdued classical style used at Williton suggests a severe, respectable, worthy establishment apparently well lit and comfortable. This belies the truth, for conditions and treatment tended to be hard, for poverty was considered a sin. Other architectural styles were used, Gothic and Jacobean, for instance, but plain classical was the most common and no doubt the cheapest. Many workhouses survived, usually through conversion to hospital use after their closure as workhouses subsequent to the introduction of unemployment benefit in 1929, but they are now threatened again. Williton has already closed and its future remains uncertain.

Tolpuddle, the tombstone of James Hammett by Eric Gill. BTA/ETB

89

8

Agriculture and Industry

The history of agricultural change is one of new methods and technology destroying the relics of the previous system. It is the oldest industry, but the pace of change since the Second World War – with more powerful tractors, deep ploughing, amalgamation of fields and loss of hedgerows – has meant that more of the archaeology of agriculture has been destroyed in the last four decades than in all the preceding centuries. Evidence of the beginnings of agriculture has been found during excavation of long barrows, the original land surface showing signs of the clearing and burning of forest, plough marks, and early grain types. It was not until the 1st century BC that the heavier ironshod plough, brought from Gaul by the Belgae, really began to shape the land in a way that can still be recognised. Some of the earliest fields still survive on the chalk lands where they have been protected from later ploughing, often in association with the hillforts, where grain storage pits and postholes of wooden granaries have been discovered. Though these 'Celtic fields' are sometimes associated with settlements of the Romano-British period, they always appear to be part of the native rather than Roman tradition. Celtic fields are different from strip lynchets in appearance and use, but the latter may be part of the same agricultural system or a development of it. They survive in fair numbers on the chalk downlands, particularly on the steep slopes where later ploughing has never taken place. There is a particularly well preserved set at **Mere** (90, W). Many of these field systems continued in use through the Dark Ages and the medieval period, but under the Normans the open-field systems, which can still be recognised all over midland England, were fully developed from their Saxon beginnings.

Open fields, cultivated continuously since the Middle Ages, still survive in a sort of use at **Portland** (91, D) and at Westcote (G). Outside the region, the fields at Laxton in Nottinghamshire, which are in the ownership of the Crown Estates Commissioners, are maintained as a piece of living history, an example of the techniques of past agricultural practice. The Great Field at Braunton in north Devon is also still maintained in the traditional form despite some simplification of landownership and amalgamation of strips. Village fields, usually three or four, can often still be recognised in areas of pastureland, with the ridge and furrow radiating out from the built-up centre, and it can be seen particularly well in places where a medieval village has been removed and the fields incorporated in a 'Capability' Brown park landscape, thus preserving them unploughed. The open-field system was widespread throughout the area on the lower lying land but should not be confused with the remains of another system in Dorset, that of the water-meadows in the flat-bottomed river valleys. These fields were irrigated through water channels and sluices so that they could be flooded in spring to provide an early growth of lush pasture. The ploughed-out remains of ridge and furrow can also be confused with modern field drainage systems which leave indentations in the ground. The best way to see ridge and furrow is from an embankment in the evening when the low sun casts clearly defined shadows from the ridges. The fields were used to rotate crops, grain, roots and then fallow, say, with the animals regularly allowed in to manure them. Each field was planted with one crop but the strips were used by different people.

The open-field system began to be replaced during the 16th century as sheep flocks were increased with the boom in the wool market, and some people were driven from the land, in very much the same way as they were in the Scottish Highland clearances three centuries later. The impact on the landscape was not great at this time, for the sheep were put mostly on the sheep walks on the high Cotswolds, on the

Glastonbury Abbey Barn. BTA/ETB

Mendips and the chalk downs of Wiltshire and Dorset, replacing some of the remaining ancient fields rather than the medieval ones in the valleys. Full-scale Parliamentary enclosure followed in the 18th century, and was largely completed by 1840 (see entry 85). It was this that produced the characteristic pattern of mainly rectangular fields surrounded by stone walls or hedgerows. It was a complex business to undertake, involving the exchange of holdings, and only wealthy landowners could afford the investment in the necessary agricultural infrastructure of field boundaries, barns, foldyards, roads and new farmhouses. It was this that gave the area the appearance it largely still has today, though the post-war period has brought new concerns such as the further erosion of Exmoor and other surviving open areas, the extraction of peat from the Somerset levels, the reafforestation of Dean with too many conifers, the destruction of dry-stone walling on the limestone hills, and the continued presence of the army on large areas of Salisbury Plain (W) and the Dorset coast.

The barn is the largest and most impressive agricultural building type, and the region is particularly rich in fine stone examples. Timber-framed barns are to be found on the northern fringes of Gloucestershire and in Wiltshire, notably the 17th-century one at Avebury (W). The great monastic barns, such as **Glastonbury Abbey Barn** (88, S), have been called 'cathedrals of the land' and not without reason. The greatest of all, at Abbotsbury (D), was 262 ft long when complete and is still impressive enough, while those at Stanway (G) and Bradford-on-Avon (W), both dating from the 14th century, have magnificent raised cruck roofs and are splendid buildings in every way. The characteristic feature of medieval barns is the row of stepped buttresses along the walls; Frocester (G) has these and so do Pilton, Doulting and Wells (all in Somerset). Tisbury (W) has an immensely long thatched barn dating from the 15th century. The Cotswold enclosure barns and outfarms, with their simple rectangular shapes and their high gabled porches, contribute

enormously to many farm and village groups and punctuate the skyline on the wold.

Granaries, dovecotes and other agricultural buildings are familiar and attractive features of these 18th-century farm groups, which often have a good farmhouse as well. Many of these groups are at risk from conversion to dwellings, which seems to be happening in almost every parish. It is very important that buildings remain in use, but if the use destroys their character, appearance and historic value then the exercise is a failure.

The economy of the area has always been based on agriculture and the majority of historic industrial buildings relate to agricultural production. The most widespread industrial buildings are corn mills, water driven, though windmills were once more common than they are today. A great many examples of water mills survive with or without machinery, but the example chosen, **Clapton Mill** (84, S) is not only absolutely complete, but also presents an almost unaltered Victorian working environment. There are three complete windmills in the region, High Ham, with its thatched roof, and Aller, both in Somerset, and Wilton Mill on the Wiltshire–Berkshire border. There is also an example of a large steam mill in Gloucester docks where it forms part of an important group of mid 19th-century warehouses.

Woollen mills are the next significant group of buildings, for this area was long famous for woollen cloth, and it is still produced at some sites even now. One of the main areas was the Stroud valley where many fine 17th- and 18th-century mills and millowners' houses can be found. West Wiltshire has large mills at Bradford-on-Avon and Trowbridge as well as many fine clothiers' houses, and there is a further group of mills around Wotton-under-Edge (G) powered by the streams running down off the Cotswold escarpment. The most significant individual buildings are **King's Stanley** (89, G), Avon Mill at Bradford (W), New Mill at Wotton and the multiphase Dunkirk Mill at Nailsworth (G). An important initiative in reuse is currently being undertaken by the Stroud Valley

Mills project while the fine Ebley Mill (G) is Stroud District Council's new offices. Two other distinctive building types relating to this industry are 'stoves' for cloth drying and shrinking, examples of which survive in the Stroud Valley and at Frome (S), and teasel houses for drying the teasels used in finishing the cloth which can be found at Trowbridge and Shepton Mallet (S).

The other extensive surviving industry is stone mining and quarrying. The Mendip area has enormous roadstone quarries at Cheddar, Wells and near Frome. Building stone of the Bath type is mined in the Avon valley, Portland white limestone is quarried on Portland, and Cotswold stone at several sites in that area. Few buildings of importance relating to this industry survive. Coal mining was once extensive in the area surrounding Bristol (A) and in the Forest of Dean (G) but the last mine, at Radstock (A), was closed in 1979. There are a number of villages in both areas which have the recognisable appearance of mining communities, particularly Radstock itself, and the Bristol map shows many names, such as California, probably derived from a mining background. There are several surviving winding houses, for example that at Lightmoor in the Forest of Dean and a Cornish type on the Brendon Hills in Somerset, the latter having been part of a lead mine.

Bristol is the only large industrial city in the region, and even there industrial activity has taken second place to that of trade. The sugar industry was strong in the 18th century and a refinery of the period has been identified at Lewins Mead. The tobacco industry is still powerful – with Wills' very fine factory as one of the area's most significant modern buildings – and its bonded warehouses still dominate the docks.

Food processing is also important in the area, with large factories like Babycham at Shepton Mallet, and Walls Ice Cream in Gloucester. The Great Western Railway Locomotive and Carriage Works at Swindon were finally closed in 1986, but an important group of Victorian industrial buildings survives and is seeking reuse. The finest modern industrial building is the Renault factory at Swindon, designed by Norman Foster. Finally there are four nuclear power stations, Hinckley Point (S), Berkeley (G) and Winfrith (D), where the early Magnox reactors will soon be closed down, and Oldbury-on-Severn (A) where this has already taken place.

84

Clapton Mill, Somerset
1864

ST 414064. 2 miles SW of Crewkerne on B3165
[B]

Clapton Mill is a survival from another age: a complete Victorian working environment still in use, producing high-grade flour milled with the original machinery (apart from appropriate new parts), and using only water power, except in periods of drought when the drive is supplemented by a Rushton & Hornsby diesel engine installed in 1931. The reason for this mill's survival in so complete a state lies in its ownership by the Lockyers, who leased it in 1870, bought it in 1901, and have continued to run it ever since, using only family labour. As a self-employed family business, the mill has managed to escape the strictures of the Factory Acts and the Health and Safety Officer. The true flavour of the past can still be experienced.

The site is a very old one, dating back to the 12th century, but the present mill was newly built in 1864 of coursed local stone with Hamstone ashlar dressings and a Welsh slate roof. The exterior is simple and unremarkable, but together with the adjacent contemporary miller's house it makes for a pleasant group. The immediate feature of interest is the iron launder carried on tall brick piers to the side of the mill, while the way the mill looms right above the road demonstrates how the carts were loaded directly in and out of the doors. The inside belies the tidy exterior with sacks, heaps and dust all about. The heavy timber and iron construction shows the weight of the machinery and the corn

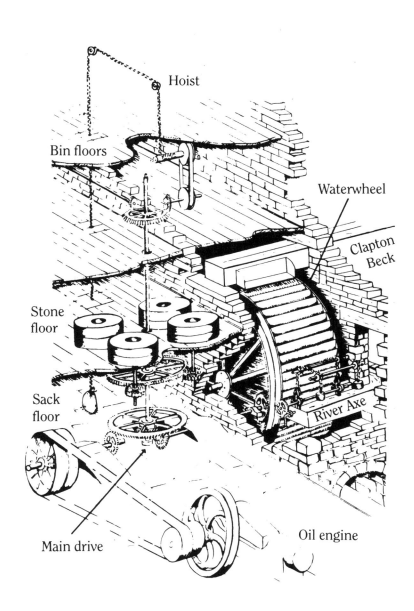

The workings of Clapton Mill, showing the alternative water sources. Lockyer & Son

itself. The arrangement is fairly standard, the top 'bin' floor with ten bins for up to 80 tons of grain and the doors to the external hoist, the 'stone' floor where the grinding takes places and the 'sack' floor where the sacks are filled and dispatched. The iron water wheel, over 3 metres in diameter, is behind the mill

and is unique for being fed twice, overshot from the launder and breast shot from the River Axe flowing across the fields on the higher ground at the rear of the building. Clapton is a most interesting survival, which is safe while it remains profitable, but could so easily vanish.

Vale of Severn enclosure fields. MR

85

Cotswolds and Vale of Severn Enclosure Fields, Gloucestershire
18th century

[D]

The immediate difference between the enclosures of the high limestone Cotswolds and those in the clay Vale is in the actual method employed. The dry-stone walls of the hills were built from the stone which would be picked from any field, and indeed had to be before it could become successful arable. In the Vale there are hedges of thorn and hazel (drastically altered by the death of every hedgerow elm in the 1970s). Both have been sadly depleted by the amalgamation of fields brought about by modern agricultural practices. The enclosures were mostly undertaken in the period 1770–1830, turning the Cotswolds from unfenced sheep walks into arable – which the visitor may see on the high wold between Northleach and Cirencester; and the Vale from open fields (the bones of which can still be seen everywhere) to pasture – to be seen, for example, from the Cotswold escarpment at Nympsfield Beacon. In the whole county of Gloucestershire only a few of these strips with thin grass balks between survive to the present day, at Westcote, where the land dips down to Oxfordshire. Enclosures brought lasting change to the appearance of the countryside and to the rural population, much of which moved to the industrial towns, leaving many rural buildings to decay. At the same time it produced the

Cotswold field barns, the out-farms, and the 18th-century farm groups which are so characteristic of the area today.

William Cobbett, who was not in favour of rural change, described the area north of Cirencester in the 1820s: 'I came up hill into a country apparently formerly a down or common, but now divided into large fields by stone walls. Anything so ugly I have never seen before. The stone . . . here lies very near the surface. The plough is continually bring [*sic*] it up, and thus, in general, came the means of making the walls. Anything quite so cheerless as this I do not recollect to have seen . . . these stones are quite abominable.' He found the enclosed fields and orchards of the Vale much more pleasing: 'All here is fine, fine farms, fine pastures, all enclosed fields, all divided by hedges, orchards a plenty.' The last word can be left to Lewis Carroll who, when staying at Cheltenham, climbed Crickley Hill and looked out over Gloucester as Cobbett had done before him, and wrote: 'A most curious country it was . . . "I declare its marked out like a large chess board!" Alice said at last' (*Through the Looking Glass and What Alice Found There*). This must be a reference to the

Severn Vale – for is not the fifth square mostly water and the seventh all forest!

86

Donnington Brewery, Gloucestershire
Late 18th–mid-19th century

SP 174272. 2 miles N of Stow-on-the-Wold between A424 and A429

[D]

The tradition of rural brewing is continued at Donnington where a tiny independent company, run by the same family since 1865, brews high quality beer on a small scale. The brewery took over an existing mill and malting on the site, and has been supplying some twenty-five public houses in the immediate area. The surviving buildings – malthouse, brewhouse, mill and miller's house – are all more or less of the same date, and very much the same character, built of coursed Cotswold stone with stone slate roofs (some now artificial). At first water provided the power for the working of the hoists, pumps and the mash tun, but steam

Donnington Brewery, the kilns and millpond from the west. MR

power was introduced later, and now only an overshot wheel survives. The picturesque cluster of buildings with its long low outline still evokes the pre-industrial age – once brewing became a large-scale industry in town centres, demand for land triggered a change to taller premises, producing the tower-type brewery of the late 19th century, such as Wadworth's Northgate Brewery in Devizes (W) and Hall & Woodhouse at Blandford (D). The reason for Donnington's situation is of course the water supply. The nearby town of Stow-on-the-Wold, where most of the beer was drunk, is waterless, and the brewery stands well down the hill near the source of the River Dikler, where there was plentiful water both for the brewing and to power the waterwheel. It was usual to have all the processes on site, but nowadays the malt is delivered from great industrial maltings elsewhere. Doves were kept to eat the spilled grain, and the remains of the mash, supposedly extremely nutritious, would be fed to pigs. The beer can be tried in most of the local villages but the Golden Ball in Lower Swell, a good 17th-century house, is a particular favourite. The brewery makes a charming picture when viewed from the surrounding hills and roads but there is no public access to the buildings.

Eastwood Manor Farm steading from the south. RCHME

87

Eastwood Manor Farm, Avon
1858–60

ST 578552. 1 mile E of East Harptree

[D]

The practice of large-scale, or 'high' farming really gripped the imagination of the English landowner when Prince Albert declared his interest in it, and began to publish his ideas, putting much of it into practice on the home farm in Windsor Great Park. With the beginnings of intensive stock rearing in the 18th century, led by Robert Bakewell and the Earl of Leicester, and the amalgamation of holdings, herds and flocks were becoming larger. By the 19th century there was a need to find

new methods of livestock management, and Eastwood Manor Farm developed from these ideas. It was built in 1858–60 to encompass every farm use under one roof: the housing and management of livestock, the storage of fodder and produce, the collection of slurry, as well as veterinary, farrier, coachhouse, blacksmith and carpenter and more. The holding in 1858 was 900 acres, and the building itself covers 1¼ acres with two large rectangular covered yards roofed with iron and glass, surrounded by complete ranges of buildings housing the uses already mentioned, as well as the great barn, with processing machinery powered by both a 27½ ft-diameter waterwheel, and a steam engine. From the outside the building looks like a railway station with its twin arched roofs. It is still used, though not to capacity, for the farm is now only 300 acres, but the water and slurry gravity systems still work as before, and the building is very largely unaltered from its original appearance.

The period 1840 until the slump in the 1880s was a golden age for British farming, with landowners taking an immense pride in the quality and breeding of their beasts and in a much

greater professionalism in all aspects of the industry. Eastwood is a very significant building and even in its present diminished use is well worth keeping.

88

Glastonbury Abbey Barn, Somerset
c.1340

ST 504385. At S end of Glastonbury, on A361 to Shepton Mallet

[A]

Glastonbury Abbey Barn represents an important aspect of the medieval economy and is a survival of the architectural heritage of the period that is less rare than one might suppose. Built to the same scale and quality of design as many a church, such barns have survived through continued use into the present day, and it is only with 20th-century changes in agricultural practices that they have become redundant. Their architectural quality has not been ignored in the past: Glastonbury Barn was illustrated by Pugin in his *Examples of Gothic*

Architecture (1830), which was used as a sourcebook for the mid 19th-century Gothic Revival. We now see them as major buildings and not just as the picturesque relics described by Thomas Hardy in *Far from the Madding Crowd*.

There is no documentation for the building of this barn but it is stylistically characteristic of the 14th century and this has been confirmed by dendrochronology (dating by counting the growth rings of trees). A likely date seems to be *c*.1340 which puts it rather earlier than the basically similar but larger and sturdier barn at Bradford-on-Avon (W). Glastonbury is a very highly finished building with beautifully cut and constructed stonework, carefully designed buttresses and gables, and decorative carving on the gable windows and finials. It is a building which speaks of the wealth and confidence of the monastic world, and was designed to store the payments in kind collected from the abbey's widespread estates. The porch, with the tally or steward's room over, leads to the threshing floor with the second porch opposite. On either side are the storage bays, and over all the magnificent roof, with two tiers of crucks and much wind bracing, which were found necessary for the wide span of 33⅓ ft. During the full restoration of the building in 1978 some 30 per cent of the roof timbers were replaced, but the

form is unchanged. Other monastic barns in the area are at Bradford-on-Avon and Abbotsbury (D), while there is a fine 15th-century manor barn at Tisbury (W) which retains its thatched roof.

89
King's Stanley Mill, Gloucestershire
1813

SO 813043. 2 miles W of Stroud to S of A419

[D]

This is one of the earliest and architecturally one of the finest of the 'fireproof' textile mills, and has remained in its original use until the present day. Already an established business, in 1813 the mill was entirely rebuilt on a grand scale. The five-storey main block is built in warm red brick with an internal structure of cast-iron columns and arches supporting brick-jack arches with stone paving laid on top. This combination of fireproof materials was supposed to combat the real danger of serious conflagration caused by the machinery and the large quantities of flammable materials, but was unlikely to have been as effective as it appeared because a fire of any

King's Stanley Mill, main block with venetian windows. MR

intensity on the lower floors would fracture the cast iron and the weight of the floors above would then bring about a progressive collapse. This one has survived, however, and is a handsome building of austere design, with rows of cast-iron mill windows, varied by the inclusion of some Venetian windows. It is in a picturesque location beside two waterways: the River Frome which powered the five waterwheels until 1959, and the Stroudwater Canal which brought coal for the steam engines (first installed in 1820) and took away the finished cloth. The internal appearance is splendid with its double rows of columns marching along the wide loom floors. The offices and ancillary buildings around the mill complete a very satisfying group of industrial buildings.

90
Mere Strip Lynchets, Wiltshire
Roman–medieval

ST 822333. In angle of A303 and B3095, 1 mile E of Mere

[D]

The face of the Wessex chalklands is marked by the remains of an agricultural system which became redundant long ago. These are the strip

Glastonbury Abbey Barn from the north. Engraving from Collinson's *History of Antiquities of Somerset*, 1791.

lynchets which may well have originated in the Romano-British period, and then continued in use during the Middle Ages, from whence they traditionally date. They have survived because they are confined to the thin chalk soils, while the improved agricultural practices of the medieval period were centred on the heavier and more productive lowland soils where the Saxons chose to found their settlements. The best examples are on the steepest slopes, as these were not ploughed in later years.

A possibly Romano-British date is suggested by inhumations of the period which have been found in the clearly pre-existing banks of some lynchets, but not at Mere. Any particular example of lynchets without such evidence may, however, be purely medieval. If they are early they could have been sited within the defensive orbit of a camp, and above the forest lands; or, if late, it may just be that they were marginal land being brought into cultivation. It remains uncertain.

The terracing of the steep hillsides was partly produced by the natural downhill movement of soil resulting from the use of the primitive ploughs, but in any case moving earth was clearly no problem to early folk who must have spent a significant proportion of their time so doing. Air photography has resulted in the identification of many such field systems, often badly damaged or ploughed out, but the Wessex chalklands still have many sites readily visible.

Mere has one of the finest sets of lynchets, occupying the steep sides of an indented edge of downland in the junction between the Warminster and Salisbury roads. The flat bottoms have been cultivated and many of the flat tops of the spurs have also been ploughed at various times, but the steepness of the slopes between have resulted in an exceptionally well preserved pattern of strips.

Mere strip-lynchets, looking south-east. RCHME

Portland open fields, showing the 'balks'. RCHME

91

Portland Open Fields, Dorset
Medieval–present day

SY 682692. On Isle of Portland, between Easton and Portland Bill

[D]

Open arable fields once covered large areas of southern England and are still readily recognisable. Traditionally the form of agriculture used in the feudal period, they had their origins in the Saxon system and developed through the Middle Ages with the increase in population and colonisation of further tracts of land. The Black Death in the 14th century is usually cited as the reason this spread was put into reverse, but the end of the system as a whole was caused by the enclosure of the best agricultural land, firstly in the Tudor period, and finally in the 18th century. The later Middle Ages also saw an enormous increase in sheep rearing encouraged by cloth export. Consequently, many open fields were made into sheep walks and whole

villages depopulated (e.g., Sheldon Manor, 58, W). By 1840 a whole system had passed away, leaving only two working examples in the region. On the Isle of Portland a total of about 150 acres remain with the cultivated strips divided by grass causeways or 'balks', appearing more like allotments than fields. For hundreds of years Portland's principal concern has been the quarrying of building stone from beneath the fields and quarrymen have had opportunities for small-scale cultivation in a way that was also traditional with coal miners in the north or the tin miners in Cornwall. This open-field system is characteristic of thin soils, and can also be found at Westcote in Gloucestershire. The heavier lowland soils, particularly in mid-England, led to the better-known corduroy appearance of 'ridge and furrow' where the strips, being ploughed individually, became mounded up, leaving the furrows between to act as drains. This is the system still partly in use at Laxton in Nottinghamshire and on Braunton Great Field in Devon, though the land holdings have been much simplified.

Ridge and furrow can be seen particularly well in our area in the Vale of Gloucester, from the embankments of the Bristol to Birmingham railway line, and also in north Wiltshire from the Bristol to London line, but are common in the river valleys, though often much damaged and obscured by later ploughing. It is particularly interesting to note strips running in different directions, maybe marking the boundaries of the different fields.

92

St Vincent's Works, Bristol, Avon
c.1883–1891

ST 603725. ½ mile E of Temple Meads station

[D]

This area is not rich in industrial buildings and certainly has little to offer in the way of heavy industry. The modern industrial landscape can be found at Avonmouth (A) where petrochemicals and metal smelting have not added to visual amenity, but a traditional industrial scene can be experienced along the River Avon and

St Vincent's Works, the Romanesque-style office block. MR

the Feeder Canal in Bristol itself. Crew's Hole, an evocatively named riverside area in east Bristol, has charm and character of a kind, but no architecture to compare with the St Vincent's Works of the Bristol Iron Company which is closer to the city centre. Established quite early in the 19th century, the works' main product was galvanised iron sheeting, still to be seen all over the city, and it entered a period of expansion following the company's takeover by John Lysaght in 1860. In the 1880s the enormous increase in the demand for galvanised sheeting in the colonies (it was for instance the traditional building material of the Australian outback where there were no local manufacturers until after the First World War) led to the building of a new works designed by the owner's brother, T R Lysaght.

The galvanising shop still stands, built attractively in the local Pennant stone with a clock facing the factory yard. Much more surprising, however, is the office building which dates from 1891, and is signed by R M Drake, though it would also appear to be the design of Lysaght. It is a sort of Walt Disney neo-Norman castle with round arches, arrow slits and conical copper roofs. Flanked by Norman arched gateways it makes a humorous and effective addition to the street, and contrasts with the bulk of the gasholders in Gas Lane, immediately to the right. This corner of Bristol is definitely off the tourist route but has a character all of its own, and it is pleasant to think of all those galvanised sheets being sent out from here to the far corners of the world.

9

Transport and Communications

The communications system of the five counties is based on ancient and modern routes passing through the area to Wales and the south-western peninsula, and beyond on to Ireland and the Americas.

The earliest roads (such as the **Ridgeway** (103, W), engineered by the feet of their users, ran along the chalk ridges which fan out from Salisbury Plain. The system appears to radiate from the great Neolithic monuments of Avebury (1, W) and Stonehenge (10, W), or these may have been sited to take advantage of already existing routes. The purposes for which ancient peoples travelled remain relatively unclear, but the flint mines at Grimes Graves in Norfolk were one incentive, the product being essential to the society of the time. The great ritual sites may have been another reason, but the trackways do not appear to pay particular regard to the known centres of population. Trade must have been more widespread and in greater volume than we imagine; even so the transformation of ancient roads into the rutted tracks we see today is really the work of generations of travellers since. The breakdown of the Roman system of roads in the Middle Ages meant that many of the older tracks, sticking to the drier high ground, continued in use, and it was during that period of wheeled traffic that the branching 'zones of movement' formed which make such striking patterns on the chalk hillsides. These ancient roads were then used for cattle droving in the 18th and 19th centuries, when movements of large groups of animals became necessary for feeding the towns and the old 'green' ways were more suitable than the paved turnpikes where the traffic would be held up, and where the drover was required to pay for right of passage.

The Roman road system which overlaid and occasionally incorporated the earlier trackways developed rapidly following the Claudian invasion of Britain in 43 AD. Fanning out first from Richborough (near Margate in Kent),

the port of entry, and then from London, the main routes in the region were the road to Dorchester and on into Devon, the Bath road, and the road to Gloucester. They were designed for the rapid deployment of troops, the encouragement of trade and the ease of the Roman colonial administrators who were thus enabled to carry out their business. They were engineered by local forces under military control using local labour and materials. Roman road surfaces and examples of construction techniques survive in many places, and in great variety depending upon the quality of the available materials. The most common characteristics of the engineering of Roman roads are described in the **Fosseway** entry (98). The Roman system continued to grow and develop firstly as the frontiers were pushed west and north, and then with the relocation of population and the growth of the towns and cities bringing new reasons for trade and travel. The imperial courier service for carrying messages to and from Rome and between provincial centres also used the roads as did the posting system for official travellers staying in the *mansio* or official inns in the same way that coaching inns were used in the 18th century, though a closer comparison could be drawn with the system for official travel in Napoleonic France.

With the end of the Roman period the roads began to become more dangerous places since the invaders could move along them quickly, and once the legions had gone the retreat away from them began. The Dark Ages saw the Roman system fall into disrepair; the Saxons avoided the roads and founded their settlements on the spring line under the hills, a landscape characteristic still very evident today. Trade continued, but goods must have been largely carried on the backs of pack horses, as throughout the Middle Ages, so a good road surface was no longer of such importance and little attention was given to road maintenance. There were

Tarr Steps, an early morning in Spring. MR

101

various enactments concerning the clearance of forest on either side of main routes to make brigandage more difficult. The Crown saw itself as responsible for the King's Highway, but did little of practical use, any cursory repairs being left to the parishes through which a road ran, and these would have been minimal indeed. There are no medieval roads surviving in anything like their used state – those still in use are tarmacked, while the greenways are not used enough to give an authentic effect. Road repair was formalised as a parish function in Elizabeth I's reign, but it was the 17th century which saw the next advance, the beginnings of the turnpike system with the first Act in 1667. The first road atlas by John Ogilby in 1675 greatly improved knowledge of the road system of the time and his strip maps record routes which are still readily identifiable today. During the following 150 years all the main routes were turnpiked, and existing roads rebuilt with better foundations and drainage and construction of an even surface of small stones, all broken by hand. These roads were provided by private trusts whose shareholders paid for the work and they were empowered to charge tolls for their use. Road engineering improved in quality and design until two systems emerged, that of Thomas Telford which must be looked for in other areas, and that of John McAdam who, with his family, took over the management of many of the trusts in the Bristol and Bath area (see **Black Dog Turnpike Road**, 93, A, W). This system of improved communication remains the basis of the A-roads of today, and only the M4, M5 and dual carriageways of the A303 and various by-passes, plus the addition of tarmacadam to the surfaces of the old roads, have really altered this in the present century.

The road and rail systems of the five counties continue to use bridges of all ages and types and four examples have been chosen to give some idea of the range. The ancient bridges constructed with simple slabs or 'clappers' demonstrate the most basic of all bridging techniques, certainly used by ancient peoples and everyone since.

Kennet and Avon Canal, Caen Hill flight of locks from the bottom bridge. MR

They have generally been rebuilt several times and could be of almost any date. There are no Roman bridge remains surviving in the area. The medieval stone bridges are exemplified by **Sturminster Newton Bridge** (105, D), one of a number – Chew Bridge, Chew Magna (A), White Mill Bridge near Sturminster Marshall (D), King John's Bridge in Tewkesbury (G) and Town Bridge, Bradford-on-Avon (W) amongst many others – which survive from the period in a more or less rebuilt and repaired state. The ones that have been incorporated into the A-road system have suffered most. Many bridges were constructed in the 18th century to replace existing ones, or as new crossings. The turnpike system gave a new sense of planning and purpose to the roads and much more ambitious engineering was attempted. **The Mythe Bridge** (108, G) near Tewkesbury, is an example of both a major turnpike bridge and a major metal bridge. Iron and later steel were to be increasingly used for bridges, particularly in the railway system. Engineering daring was a feature of the 19th century, and the **Clifton Suspension Bridge** (96, A) exemplifies both a new technique and the work of the great engineer Brunel, who was particularly associated with the region. Severn Bridge, completed in 1966, is the largest example of this development, but Clifton Bridge is proving more resilient after 130 years than the Severn after its meagre twenty-five.

Two major canals across England are included: the **Thames and Severn Canal** (104, G) now derelict, and the **Kennet and Avon Canal** (97, A, W) which is now

fully navigable once more. The **Gloucester–Sharpness Canal** (100, G), a ship canal to Gloucester Docks, is also featured. There are others and, of those in use, the Bridgwater Canal (S) and the Grand Western Canal near Taunton (S) are the most interesting, but the derelict ones also have surviving features which the keen visitor can seek out. The Wiltshire and Berkshire Canal, the Chard Canal, the Hereford Canal are all such ones, and they run through attractive scenery.

The two major dock systems of **Bristol Floating Harbour** (94, A) and **Gloucester Docks** (100, G) are by far the most interesting, but there are also a number of relatively minor ports on both coasts: Christchurch and Poole with their fine natural harbours, Lyme Regis (D), Bridgwater (S), Portishead (A) and Watchet (S) are all still in use to some degree though mostly for fishing or leisure. Small traditional, largely 18th-century harbours survive at Watchet and Minehead (S) while the Cobb at Lyme Regis, famous for its literary associations (Jane Austen's *Persuasion* and John Fowles's *The French Lieutenant's Woman*) is the best example on the Dorset coast. The cross-channel packet trade is represented by Weymouth and Poole (D) while there are 19th-century railway docks at Bridgwater (S) and Portishead (A). Sharpness (G) and Gloucester are the result of the river trade on the Severn and beyond, while the Forest of Dean coalfield had its outlet through Lydney (G, still in use) and Bullo Pill (G). The only modern dock system is that at Avonmouth, developed when the size of ships in the 19th century began to make the approach to Bristol impossible, but the decline of trade with the Americas in the present century has meant that this has never really become a key British port. There are pleasure piers at Bournemouth (D), Weston-super-Mare (A) and **Clevedon** (95, S). The only really significant dry dock and historic ship is included, the **Great Western Dry Dock and SS *Great Britain*** (101, A).

The railway system of the area radiates from two centres, Bristol (A) and Salisbury (W), and was controlled by two main companies, the Great Western and the London South Western, though the Midland and the Somerset & Dorset also had important lines running from north to south which are now almost completely taken up. The **Great Western Railway** (102, A, W) was inaugurated at Bristol in 1835 and the first section between Bristol and Bath opened in 1840. Before it opened all the way to London in 1841, two lesser lines from Bristol had already been completed. The Birmingham and Gloucester line engineered by Captain Moorsom was opened in 1840. It included the Lickey Bank, 2 miles at a gradient of 1 in 37 up the escarpment above Bromsgrove, which remains very similar to when it was opened, and still gives pause to the heavier trains, though banking engines are no longer required. All the original stations have gone except the sadly damaged Cheltenham Spa (originally Lansdown Road). The Bristol to Gloucester line was engineered by Brunel, but only wayside fragments remain, together with Wickwar tunnel. To the south the Bristol and Exeter Railway, also by Brunel, was opened in part the same day as the Great Western, but not completely until 1844. Yatton (A), Bridgwater and Taunton (S) retain all or part of their original stations. There is also the Avon Valley line to Westbury (W) and Salisbury with a good original station at Bradford-on-Avon (W), as well as the branch to Castle Cary (S) and Weymouth with the important station at **Frome** (99, S).

The London & South Western Railway enters the area at Christchurch (D) and runs through to Weymouth with a longer and later line running through Salisbury, Sherborne (D) and Crewkerne (S) and on to Devon and eventually Cornwall. The surviving stations by the company architect Sir William Tite can be found at Salisbury (1859), which is in his Italianate manner, and Crewkerne (1859) in the Tudor Gothic which he adopted in his later years. Of later stations the monumental Bournemouth Central (1855) is worth visiting, though many people may find it not to their taste. Of later lines the principal one is the Great Western 'cut-off' from Westbury to Taunton designed to shorten the journey from London to the

far west from the Great Way Round via Bristol to meet the London & South Western challenge. Opened in 1906, it is utilitarian in the extreme.

93
Black Dog Turnpike Road, Avon and Wiltshire
1834

ST 780620. A36 Bath–Warminster trunk road
[C]

By the mid-1820s the family of John Loudon McAdam had the road system of south Gloucestershire, north Somerset and west Wiltshire entirely within their engineering control, 340 continuous miles of Macadamised road. J L McAdam, the 'Colossus of Roads', gave the Bath area the best constructed and managed turnpike system in the country, while also producing good profits for the trustees and shareholders. The McAdam system was based on thorough construction, careful supervision and regular maintenance. The key to its success was the care with which the stone was broken: the smaller

it was the better it bonded together, for ruts would form almost immediately if the stones were too large. McAdam recommended breaking so that the stone would pass through an inch screen.

The Black Dog Trust, called after the public house in which the trustees met, was a small trust with roads running between Bath, Warminster and Frome, which joined up to roads built by the trusts of those towns. William McAdam, John's son, was appointed surveyor to the trust in 1819, and in 1832 was put in charge of the construction of a new stretch of road between Bath and Beckington (S). But he was a difficult man, and was replaced by his son William junior who carried through the construction of the road and remained employed by the Black Dog Trust until his death in 1861. The road runs along the Avon valley by the Kennet and Avon Canal (see entry 97), crossing the handsome eleven-arch viaduct at Limpley Stoke (designed by G P Manners) and climbing up out of the valley to Hinton Charterhouse along a twisting line but well-engineered gradient. This road was to be built despite the opposition of the Bath

Black Dog Turnpike Road: Limpley Stoke Viaduct from the south, with Brassknocker Hill zig-zagging up to the left. MR

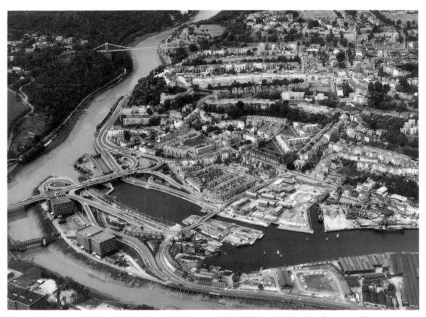

The entrance to Bristol Floating Harbour, with Clifton in the background. CUCAP

Turnpike Trust, whose toll-gate at the foot of Brassknocker Hill would be by-passed by a better road into Bath. William McAdam somehow managed to achieve amicable discussions with the Bath Burnpike Trust's surveyors, his own father and son, during the period of planning in 1832. This was the last major road engineered in the area before the coming of the railways, when the construction traffic was to destroy their surfaces and the opening of the lines their revenue. This road is the modern A36 and remains a fine piece of work.

94

Bristol Floating Harbour, Avon
1803–1873

ST 566724–ST 590729. In city centre

[C]

Closed to commercial shipping in 1976, the Bristol Upper, or City, Docks retain much of interest, for no great alterations have been made since the 1870s. By the turn of the 20th century the size of commercial shipping was becoming inexorably too large for the bends in the River Avon, and the modern docks at Avonmouth (founded in 1877) were overtaking the City docks.

The enormous tidal range in the rivers Severn and Avon meant that Bristol could only be approached, and left, at high tide and a floating harbour became an early requirement, but was held up by the lengthy squabbles and prevarications of the dock company and the Merchant Venturers. In 1803, however, an ambitious scheme was completed to make the whole of the navigable Avon and Frome above Hotwells into a float. This was engineered by William Jessop with a by-pass or 'new cut' for the River Avon, with two entrance locks and basins to the float, Cumberland Basin in the west and Bathurst Basin in the east, of which the latter is the less altered. Cumberland Basin was improved, with enlarged locks and the underfall for silt scouring, by Brunel in the 1840s, and the present system of entrance locks was completed by Thomas Howard in 1873. Relics of all these dates survive, as do hydraulic swing bridges, a 35-ton Fairbain steam crane of 1875, the Piranesian Bush's Warehouse of the 1840s (now the Arnolfini Arts Centre) and the wonderful 'Bristol Byzantine' Welsh Back Granary of 1869. There are also early 19th-century dock workers' cottages and the Underfall Yard with its hydraulic machinery of 1871. Three enormous early 20th-century tobacco bonds at Cumberland Basin and the 1965 Cumberland Swing Bridge complete the picture.

95

Clevedon Pier, Avon
1868

ST 402719. On W side of town centre

[C]

Clevedon's pier is one of the oldest surviving pleasure piers in the country and is characteristic of the simple early type, for designs became enormously elaborate in the 1890s and 1900s. First opened on Easter Monday 1869, it was designed and constructed by J W Grover and R Ward of Westminster with the architectural embellishments added by Hans Price, a local architect and designer of the Market Hall and Royal Pier Hotel as well as several buildings in his native Weston-super-Mare (A).

The pier is of unusual design with a masonry approach 180 ft long and then eight 100 ft spans of iron construction, using as an economy rolled wrought-iron Barlow rails of the type used by Brunel for the South Wales Railway. These had been invented by William Barlow in 1848. They are riveted back to back to form round-headed arches

This 1890 view of Clevedon Pier has changed little. SOUTH AVON MERCURY

which support the wooden decking. The original wooden landing stage was replaced in 1894 by an iron one set at an angle to the pier to offset the scouring effect of the tides.

This type of pier was fully developed by Eugenius Birch who designed Birnbeck Pier at Weston-super-Mare (A) (1867, ST 308624) as well as Brighton's West Pier (1863–6). These were constructed on cast-iron piles which were screwed into the sea bed, a method used for jetties of all sorts. There was a partial collapse of Clevedon Pier in 1970 when the two outermost spans could not withstand weight testing, but it has at long last been repaired and rebuilt by the Clevedon Pier Trust and was reopened in 1989, though the pierhead still awaits reconstruction. The whole appearance of Clevedon Pier is extremely decorative and adds to its setting in the sweep of Clevedon Bay. The enormous tidal range of the Bristol Channel, however, does mean that there never seems to be much water under the pier.

96

Clifton Suspension Bridge, Bristol, Avon
1836 and 1864

ST 564731. On Clifton Downs 2 miles W of Bristol city centre

[C]

Today's bridge is almost unaltered in appearance from when it was opened in 1864, but is very different from the original Brunel design of 1836. A bridge over the Clifton Gorge had excited the Georgians' imagination for many years. A bequest of £1,000 for the purpose was made in 1753, but with a drop of 250 ft to the river it was plain that a single span was a necessity and it was not until the further development of the suspension bridge by Thomas Telford and Captain Brown in the period 1815–20 that a span of the necessary size became a real possibility. The new technology coincided with the bridge fund reaching £8,000 so an Act of Parliament was obtained and a competition held in 1829 with Telford acting as one of the assessors. The

Clifton Suspension Bridge shortly before opening in 1864, viewed from Leigh Woods with Christchurch Clifton in the background. RCHME

boldest scheme was by the 23-year-old Isambard Kingdom Brunel, aided by Thomas Rickman, who proposed a 980 ft suspension span with chains anchored directly to the rock face on either side and with the roadway emerging from a tunnel. It would truly have been a 'sublime' experience for the traveller but was rejected by Telford, who produced a curiously timid alternative with vast Gothic towers rising up from river level. The trustees asked Brunel to try again and a design in the Gothic style, later changed to Egyptian, and with the lesser span of 702 ft, was approved in 1831 and finally commenced in 1836. This was abandoned in 1840 when money ran out and the suspension chains, sold in 1849, were eventually incorporated into the Royal Albert Bridge at Saltash in Devon, the world's only railway suspension bridge. The towers stood forlorn until 1864 when the Institution of Civil Engineers chose to commemorate their dead ex-president by completing the bridge as we see it today. They re-used the suspension chains from the Hungerford Market footbridge which Brunel had also designed in 1845, and which had been demolished to build Charing Cross railway bridge, the work of John Hawkshaw who, with William Barlow, acted as engineer in the completion of the Clifton Bridge.

97

Dundas Aqueduct and Kennet and Avon Canal, Avon and Wiltshire
1796–1800

ST 786626 and ST 754644–SU 470672. On E side of A36 ½ mile N of Limpley Stoke

[C]

Named after Charles Dundas MP, chairman of the Kennet and Avon Canal Company, Dundas Aqueduct is the most impressive of the masonry structures on the Kennet and Avon Canal and perhaps the finest such bridge in England – only Telford's Welsh aqueducts really exceed it in Britain. Executed by John Rennie this monumental classical design of tremendous dignity and presence carries the canal some 60 ft above the River Avon on a wide arch spanning 65 ft, which is framed by paired giant pilasters. This central arch is flanked by smaller ones and further pilasters and then, on the west side, the embankment is pierced by a Brunel arch for the railway, put through in 1858. Built of fine quality Bath ashlar, the stonework suffered years of neglect by the canal's then owners the Great Western Railway, but this section was brought back into use by the Canal Trust in 1983 and the whole of the canal route through to Newbury, Berkshire, was reopened in 1990. The dominant architectural characteristic of the aqueduct is the enormous cornice which projects 4 ft and is an unfortunate attraction to the daring.

There is another aqueduct at Avoncliffe a few miles upstream but this is not of the same quality. The canal as a whole has many other interesting features in the area: Caen Hill Locks at Devizes (W), with twenty-nine locks, including a continuous staircase of seventeen; (SU 976614 to SU 995615), the two pumping stations of Crofton (W) with a Boulton & Watt steam engine of 1812 (SU 262623) and Claverton (A) where a waterwheel-worked pump lifts water from river to canal (ST 792644). These can all be visited.

The canal also formed a line of defence during the Second World War (see Kennet and Avon Stop-line, 16, W).

Dundas Aqueduct, the upstream side. MR

98

Fosseway
1st century AD

ST 323048–SP 223376. Follows A37 and A429 trunk roads

[C]

The Roman invasion of Britain in 43 AD was followed by a fairly rapid advance northward and westward, and the establishment of a frontier based roughly on the rivers Severn and Trent. The Fosseway, which runs from Axminster to Lincoln, was thus a key route in the process of colonisation, acting first in a military capacity to enable troops to deploy rapidly along the frontier to quell any incursions, and later to carry trade. Cirencester (G) and Lincoln were quickly established as major towns; the latter was a legionary base. Bath (A) also developed on this route and at the southern termination, near Exeter in Devon, a convenient port was developed.

As it passes through the area this road displays all the characteristics of Roman roads in an impressive state of preservation: the long straight

Fosseway from the air. CUCAP

alignments between sighting points, the zigzags up steep hills and the stretches of well defined embankment or 'agger'. Evidence of the original metalling and construction, using local materials bonded into a well drained sandwich, has often survived the centuries well. The road runs from Ilchester (S) north-west towards Bath over the Mendips, then more brokenly to Cirencester, on to Stow-on-the-Wold and Moreton-in-Marsh in Gloucestershire, and then into Warwickshire towards Leicester, Newark and Lincoln. The line is immediately apparent from the modern road map, the A37 and A429 follow it, but it also survives in every other capacity – minor road, lane, green lane, footpath and parish boundary – as later users adjusted to avoid steep climbs and boggy bottoms when the Roman surfaces eventually degenerated through lack of maintenance.

One of the best places to see it today is from the top of Wraxall Hill 4 miles south of Shepton Mallet (S) on the A37 looking south-west where a classic view, almost like that in an aerial photograph, can be obtained. It can also be followed on the minor roads to the north of Bath where there is still the feeling of frontier. Between Bath and Grittleton (W) the Fosse runs on a high ridge with the ground falling away on both sides, to prevent any possibility of ambush or surprise. In the Easton Grey area (W) it survives for long distances as a green lane, and parish and county boundary.

Its Roman origins are also apparent in some of the village names (e.g., Stratton-on-the-Fosse), and in the lack of settlements other than Roman ones on the route. The Saxons, founders of most villages, avoided these symbols of their predecessors, both for security reasons and to find suitable water supplies for their villages.

99

Frome Station, Somerset
c.*1850*

ST 784476. On E side of town to S of Warminster Rd
[C]

Frome station is now a unique survival on the British railway system. It is a through train shed constructed entirely of wood except for the iron roof ties and the corrugated roof cladding. This was once a type common to the Western Region, but is now the last, having been carefully repaired by British Rail in the late 1970s. The early railways used many wooden buildings despite the fire risk, principally for economy, but also to enable the lines to be brought quickly into use. More permanent structures could be provided once the income was assured. I K Brunel, the Chief Engineer and architect of the Great Western Railway, had an occasional sense of economy, and was also an early leader in the design of prefabricated and standardised buildings. Frome is a variation on one of his station types, designed by an assistant, J R Hannaford who was engineer to the Wells, Somerset and Weymouth Railway, which was sponsored and quickly taken over by the Great Western. It consists of a train shed across both tracks, now only one, with offices on the 'up' town side. Internally it has one aisle and wooden posts on the platform. The limited extent of the shed demonstrates the small size of early trains and is still right for today's Sprinters. All is undemonstrative design, good sense and economy. Another early Brunel station type survives at Yatton with its differing example of his 'chalet' designs on each platform, and also in the terminus at Temple Meads (107, A).

100

Gloucester Docks and Gloucester–Sharpness Canal, Gloucestershire
Docks c.*1780–1850*
Canal *1794–1827*

SO 825185 and SO 827185–SO 668033. On SW side of city centre
[C]

The dangerous nature of the currents and tides on the River Severn, particularly where it narrows and bends at Newnham, where the bore begins to build up, led to early pleas for safer passage to Gloucester and beyond. From about 1750 until the coming of the

Frome station's all-timber construction. MR

Gloucester Docks, with two of the 19th-century warehouses. EH

between sea and river boats. The influence of Telford can be seen, for the warehouse design used here originated in St Katherine's Dock, London, in the 1820s and was developed fully by Jesse Hartley at Albert Dock in Liverpool in the 1850s. The North Warehouse dates from 1826, the Pillar Warehouse from 1836 and the City Flour Mills from 1850. Immensely strong cast-iron columns, open ground floors, and partial overhang over the water for easy loading into the upper storeys are all characteristic of this important and attractive Victorian building type. The surviving warehouses, with the unaltered arrangement of locks, bridges and quays, makes Gloucester quite unique, and the council has realised that this is a resource that must not be wasted. One warehouse was burnt to the ground, but has been rebuilt; others are in use for traditional purposes, while several have found new uses: two as the headquarters of Gloucester City Council and another as the Inland Waterways Museum. The whole area is a particularly fine and attractive example of what can be done with a Victorian industrial complex.

101

Great Western Dry Dock and SS *Great Britain*, Bristol, Avon
1839–1843

ST 574724. On S side of Floating Harbour off Cumberland Rd

[A]

This is one of the most complete and evocative memorials to the great Victorian engineer Isambard Kingdom Brunel. The dock itself was designed by Brunel for the purpose of constructing his revolutionary and very large new ship, which was to be laid down, built and fitted out all on the same spot. The dock is a very good example of the dry docks of the time, with stepped sides and keel blocks and, at the river end, a single-leaf floating caisson gate originally of wrought iron, now replaced in steel. To have the SS *Great Britain* actually in the dock is most remarkable,

railways, the Severn was the best carriage route to and from the manufacturing areas centred on Birmingham and the Black Country. Engineered by Mylne and Telford, the canal was begun in 1794 but the project quickly ran out of money, and was not completed until 1827 at a cost of £444,000. Despite its mere 16½-mile length, it was then the largest ship canal in the country, taking vessels of 1,000 tons, and was heavily used, particularly by the grain and timber trades, the latter still remaining important to Gloucester.

The canal has attractive Doric lodges and wooden swingbridges but is not of special interest in engineering terms.

Sharpness Dock was enlarged in 1874 and has an office building and a warehouse of that period, but by far the most interesting are the docks at Gloucester, which were immensely busy, even in the relatively recent past. They still retain an almost complete set of 19th-century warehouses, built of brick with cast-iron columns supporting the ground floor and the interiors, and used for transferring the cargoes

as it was brought back in 1970 from the Falkland Islands where it had lain derelict since being abandoned there in 1888. The ship was launched by Prince Albert in May 1843, and, at 3,675 tons, was the largest ship then afloat. It was not the first iron ship, nor the first steam ship, nor the first of these to cross the Atlantic: it was the first ship in which screw propulsion was combined with watertight bulkheads and with the beginnings of a double skin hull and thus was the first truly modern ship, for they are constructed on the same principles to this day. Even Brunel did not entirely trust the steam engines, for six masts were also fitted, while his critics said that enough coal could not be carried to make the crossing without taking up all the space meant for passengers – no doubt with the result described by Jules Verne in *Around the World in 80 Days*.

After twenty years the ship is now approaching complete restoration, and its beauty and technical ingenuity can once again be appreciated. The adjoining office building is supposed to be the one used by Brunel to design and supervise the construction of this wonderful ship.

102

Great Western Railway, Avon and Wiltshire
1836–1841

ST 595784–SV 149856. Bristol to Swindon via Bath and Chippenham
[C]

The western, and more interesting, half of the Great Western Railway runs through the region and despite inevitable modification, and the disappearance of all the wayside stations in the 1960s, the line still retains much of its design character. It stands as a tribute to its engineer I K Brunel, and is the work which made him one of the best known men of the Victorian period.

Great Western Railway, Sydney Gardens cutting in Bath. MR

Starting from Temple Meads Station (107, A), the line runs through five tunnels, mostly with castellated entrances, to Bath and then climbs steeply up through the nearly 2-mile-long Box Tunnel and over a fine viaduct at Chippenham. After a further steep climb up Dauntsey Bank, Swindon is reached, where the great locomotive and carriage works survive in part together with the railway village (80, W), and then on to the highest point of the line as it crosses the Thames watershed into Oxfordshire. Much of the stone facings for the bridges and cuttings which gave the line such a feeling of quality, particularly in the Bath area, came from the workings themselves: Bath stone out of Box Tunnel and the grey Pennant stone used around Bristol out of Foxes Wood Tunnel.

This railway was built to a larger scale than others of its time, the permanent way being 30 ft wide (twin 7-ft tracks) and thus requiring more material and expense. Brunel's insistence on gentle gradients and curves (none less than 1 mile in radius) meant that this was always a high-speed line – the 55-mile Paddington to Didcot stretch took 47½ minutes in 1848. The line has not been electrified, thus preserving its visual character, and it was used for the introduction of the high-speed diesel service in 1976. Almost every detail, both of the engineering and the architecture, was apparently designed by Brunel himself, and it is this quality of consistency and finish which, despite the demolitions and some woeful alterations, can still inspire the visitor.

Great Western dry dock as it will never be seen again. THE SWPA PICTURE COMPANY LTD

103

Ridgeway, Wiltshire
3rd millennium BC

SV 110623–SV 193794. ½ mile E of
West Kennet on A4
[C]

The ancient road called the Ridgeway
was one of the best used of all the
pre-historic long-distance trade routes,
as finds of all kinds along the route have
shown. Its existence may also be related
to the development of Silbury Hill (8, W)
and Avebury (1, W). It runs along the
scarp of the chalk downs which cut
diagonally across central southern
England, a route that is high and dry
with good visibility and security, where
reasonably speedy travel can be achieved
at all seasons of the year.

That part of the Ridgeway which is in
our area starts south-west of
Marlborough at Alton Barnes, crosses
East Wansdyke (at SV 118649) and runs
round the Marlborough Downs to the
Iron Age hillfort of Barbury Castle (SV
146764). From there it runs north-east
past Swindon and up onto the ridge
above White Horse Vale. In Oxfordshire
it continues past the White Horse, over
the Thames at Goring and becomes the
Icknield Way on the Chiltern ridge,
leading eventually to Grimes Graves in
Norfolk, the Neolithic flint mines which

seem to have produced the principal
trade commodity for the route.

Such ancient routes were engineered
almost entirely by the feet of those that
used them, and were varied according to
the terrain and season, so they might fan
out to enormous widths as travellers
sought the driest and easiest line along
difficult stretches of the routes. This is
known as a 'zone of movement', with the
tracks fanning out and joining again,
particularly where steep slopes are
climbed. Such usage continued
throughout the Middle Ages and up to
the 18th century when these routes were
used for cattle droving. They provide a
complete contrast with the Roman roads
(see Fosseway, 98), which were
engineered for directness and tended to
disregard the contours.

It has been suggested that tumuli
were sometimes sited as waymarkers,
and many can be seen along these early
routes, notably where the A4 crosses the
Ridgeway at SV 119681.

104

Sapperton Tunnel and
Thames and Severn Canal,
Gloucestershire
1785–1789

SO 848050–SU 205988. At
Sapperton and Coates on either side
of A419, 3 miles W of Cirencester
[D]

Sapperton Tunnel was one of the
wonders of the 18th century. At 2¼
miles it was the longest tunnel in the
world, and was admired by George III
who even paid a visit to the diggings
when staying at nearby Cirencester
Park. Engineered by Robert Whitworth,
it was constructed with enormous
difficulty across the watershed and
carries the Thames and Severn Canal
through the Cotswolds into the valley of
the Frome at Sapperton, and from there
the canal drops down to Brimscombe
Port where it joins the older
Stroudwater Canal and so down to the
Severn.

It is instructive to stand at the crossroads to the south-east of Sapperton
village (SO 948027) where the spoil

Sapperton Tunnel's recently restored
southern portal. MR

heaps surrounding each working shaft
can be seen marching away over the
fields, each heap crowned with a ring of
trees. At the Thames or eastern end of
the tunnel is a fine classical ashlar
portal, recently restored by the Thames
and Severn Canal Trust, and nearby
stands the inn built as a lodging house
for the 'navigators' who dug the tunnel.
There is a plainer portal in rubble stone
at the west end and a second inn, The
Daneway, by one of the excellent stone
bridges. The tunnel had no towpath, the
narrow boats being taken through by
'leggers' who lay on outriggers and
walked their way along the tunnel wall, a
dreadfully arduous task entertainingly
described in C S Forester's *Hornblower
and the Atropos*, where it was
undertaken by the lieutenant himself.
Also worth inspecting near the east end
is the round cottage built for the
lengthman, responsible for a stretch of
canal, of which others survive at
Chalford and Lechlade in
Gloucestershire.

The tunnel also passes under the
Cheltenham and Great Western Union
Railway, built in 1845 by Brunel to link
Cheltenham and Gloucester to the Great
Western at Swindon. You are warned not
to attempt to enter the tunnel which,
together with the canal, has been
derelict since 1922.

The Ridgeway crossing Barbury Castle
south of Swindon. CUCAP

105

Sturminster Newton Bridge, Dorset
c.1500

ST 784135. On B3092 at S end of village
[C]

The invaluable record of England's bridges in the reign of Henry VIII given in John Leland's *Itinerarum* of 1545 tells us that this bridge was in existence, but it is recorded as newly built, which generally means either during the reign or very shortly before it. It has the character of a late medieval bridge of about 1500, being of stone with six pointed arches and with cutwaters on both sides. The bridge was widened in the early 19th century, no doubt when it became incorporated into the turnpike system, and two date stones probably record this: one is 1820 (and most unusually is set upside down so that it can be read easily when you lean over the parapet) and the other is 1827. The causeway extension to the bridge on the east side, with another ten semicircular arches, is also from this period and is dated 1828. The bridge demonstrates very clearly the kind of improvement which was found necessary for the turnpikes, doubled in width but with no apparent strengthening. Indeed, the careful construction and general overspecification of medieval stone bridges has meant that many have proved capable of carrying today's loads, and it is generally the widths and the cambers which have made the rebuildings necessary.

The notice on the bridge has no doubt deterred any acts of vandalism: 'Any person wilfully injuring any part of this county bridge will be guilty of felony and upon conviction liable to be transported for life by the Court.'

106

Tarr Steps, Somerset
Probably medieval

SS 868321. 3 miles S of Withypool off B3223
[C]

Tarr Steps is a mystery, because the clapper form of construction is traditionally medieval or even prehistoric in origin, but this particular bridge is on a much larger scale than any other of its type. It is known to have been rebuilt so often, and probably in every part, that today's bridge can only be an approximation of the structure even of two hundred years ago, let alone the far distant past. The River Barle, like all the Exmoor streams, is prone to sudden and violent flooding; the controversial cultivation of large areas of the moor in the 20th century has only added to this problem, and since the Second World War there have been three major repairs to the bridge (in 1948, 1953 and 1982–3 by Somerset County Council, the Royal Engineers and Exmoor National Park, respectively). Despite frequent rebuilding, it is an impressive, if rather uncertain, structure. The stream is wide (about 50 yds) and shallow, and there are seventeen spans crossed by twenty-three large flags, four being double ones. These rest on stone rubble piers which are protected by cutwaters in the form of angled stones on both the upstream and downstream sides.

There are a number of clapper bridges on Dartmoor of possibly more ancient construction, for example the incomplete one at Dartmeet, but as far as Tarr Steps is concerned some date in the Middle Ages or even later is most likely. The bridge gives an idea of what very early bridges were like. It is also very attractive, which accounts for the large numbers of visitors not necessarily interested in authentic early engineering.

Sturminster Newton Bridge, the south side. RCHME

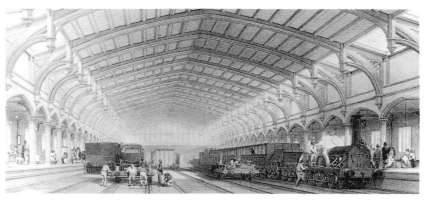

Temple Meads Station from the London end. A lithograph from J C Bourne's *History and Description of the Great Western Railway*, 1846.

107

Temple Meads Station, Bristol, Avon
1839–1935

ST 595724. ½ mile SE of city centre
[C]

The current British Rail station is not the original terminus of the Great Western Railway, but is the 1865–78 joint station for the Midland, Great Western and Bristol and Exeter railways, and was designed by Brunel's friend Matthew Digby Wyatt who had provided the architectural gloss to his Paddington Station in the 1850s. The original 1839–40 Great Western terminus is still here, having been restored in the 1980s by the Brunel Trust, and is now given over to exhibition space. It remains the least altered of the termini of the original trunk lines, and thus demonstrates what were considered the necessary qualities of planning and architecture of such a building. Brunel was helped with the design by Thomas Rickman who had earlier helped him with his competition designs for the Clifton Suspension Bridge (96, A). A three-storey ashlar-faced block in Tudor style faces the street. A carriage arch on the left was balanced by another, now gone. Passengers entered the left arch for the departure platform; and behind the front block which contains offices and the boardroom are the engine shed and the magnificent train shed with arrival and departure platforms intact, though now projecting beyond the rows of cast-iron columns which originally stood at the platforms' edges. The centre tracks were always for spare rolling stock. The whole is covered by a pseudo hammerbeam roof, of a 72 ft span, which Brunel proudly made wider than that of Westminster Hall. The shed was extended by Wyatt in the 1860s and trains were finally withdrawn from it in 1965.

The working station is in a Gothic style and once had a spire on the tower. It has a good ticket hall and refreshment room (though both are cluttered by later additions) and an iron roof on a curve spanning 125 ft, by Francis Fox, engineer to the Bristol and Exeter Railway. This roof was beautifully restored in 1990. The later platforms (by P C Culverhouse, 1935) are beyond and the Jacobean-style Bristol and Exeter office building of 1852, by S C Fripp, stands outside in the forecourt.

108

The Mythe Bridge, Gloucestershire
1826

SO 889337. 1 mile N of Tewkesbury on A438
[C]

The cast-iron arch road bridge reached its high point in terms of strength, beauty and economy of design in the later bridges of Thomas Telford, the fruit of his association with William Hazeldine, the Shrewsbury ironmaster and 'wizard of iron' whose innovative techniques produced the quality of castings which Telford's spans and specifications made necessary. In 1826 the River Severn was a commercial waterway to an extent unimaginable today and the traditional ship, the trow with its tall mast, and the dangerous nature of the river itself, meant that single spans with high clearances were a necessity. Telford, as Surveyor for Shropshire, had a long association with the river, but both the major bridges over the lower Severn in Gloucestershire – the masonry Over Bridge at Gloucester of 1827–31 and the iron Mythe Bridge at Tewkesbury – are the products of his later life when he was Britain's leading bridge engineer. The Mythe Bridge is a single cast-iron arch carried on six ribs and spans 170 ft over the river with additional flood arches on the western side.

The demands of modern traffic have meant that the decking was replaced by concrete in 1923, and there has been more recent strengthening. But though it still carries a busy road, the bridge is visually much the same as when built. The only other iron bridge to compare with it in the area is the five-arch Chepstow Bridge over the Wye designed by J U Rastrick and built in 1816, a most attractive structure which carried the A48 until 1988. The Mythe Bridge still has its attractive toll-house at the east end, also designed by Telford.

The Mythe Bridge, the downstream side viewed from the west bank. MR

Bibliography

In addition to the volumes listed below, the reader is referred to the following sources of information: statutory lists of buildings of special architectural and historic interest published by the Department of the Environment and held by the National Buildings Record, London, and the appropriate local authorities; guidebooks to the sites, particularly those by English Heritage and the National Trust; inventories of the Royal Commission on Historical Monuments for England, notably those on Dorset published by HMSO in the 1960s and 1970s; and also RCHM reports on individual buildings held in the National Buildings Record, London.

From the list below, the works of Pevsner in the Buildings of England series (Penguin) are particularly useful.

G Biddle and O S Nock, *The Railway Heritage of Britain: 150 Years of Railway Architecture and Engineering*, Michael Joseph, 1983.

H Brunel, *The Life of Isambard Kingdom Brunel, Civil Engineer*, 1870, reprinted by David & Charles, 1971.

H Colvin, *A Biographical Dictionary of British Architects, 1660–1840*, John Murray, 1978 (2nd edn).

D Cruickshank, *A Guide to the Georgian Buildings of Great Britain and Ireland*, Rizzoli, National Trust and Irish Georgian Society, 1986.

G Darley, *Villages of Vision*, Architectural Press, 1975.

K Falconer, *Guide to England's Industrial Heritage*, Batsford, 1980.

H P R Finberg, *The Gloucestershire Landscape*, Hodder & Stoughton, 1975.

L Fleming and G Gore, *The English Garden*, Michael Joseph, 1979.

M Girouard, *The Victorian Country House*, Yale, 1979.

A Gomme, M Jenner and B Little, *Bristol: An Architectural History*, Lund Humphries, 1979.

A S Gray, *Edwardian Architects: A Biographical Dictionary*, Gerald Duckworth, 1985.

A M Hadfield, *The Chartist Land Company*, David & Charles, 1970.

J Hawkes, *The Shell Guide to British Archaeology*, Michael Joseph, 1986.

W Ison, *The Georgian Buildings of Bath*, Faber & Faber, 1958.

W Ison, *The Georgian Buildings of Bristol*, Kingsmead, 1978.

D Jacques, *Georgian Gardens: The Reign of Nature*, Batsford, 1983.

E T Macdermot, *History of the Great Western Railway* (revised by C R Clinker), Ian Allan, 1964.

C Malone, *Avebury*, Batsford and English Heritage, 1989.

R Muir, *History from the Air*, Michael Joseph, 1983.

N Pevsner, *A History of Building Types*, Thames & Hudson, 1976.

N Pevsner, *North Somerset and Bristol*, Penguin, 1958.

N Pevsner, *Wiltshire*, Penguin, 1975 (2nd edn).

N Pevsner and J Newman, *Dorset*, Penguin, 1972.

N Pevsner and D Verey, *The Cotswolds*, Penguin, 1979 (2nd edn).

N Pevsner and D Verey, *The Vale and Forest of Dean*, Penguin, 1976 (2nd edn).

A Pugsley (ed.), *The Works of Isambard Kingdom Brunel*, University of Bristol, 1976.

W J Read, *Macadam, the McAdam family and the Turnpike Roads, 1798–1861*, Heinemann, 1980.

M Seaborne, *The English School: Its Architecture and Organization, 1370–1870*, Routledge & Kegan Paul, 1971.

W J Sivewright, *Civil Engineering Heritage: Wales and West of England*, Thomas Telford, 1986.

N Thomas, *A Guide to Prehistoric England*, Batsford, 1960.

M Wood, *The English Medieval House*, Ferndale, 1981.

Index

Index by Madaleine Combie

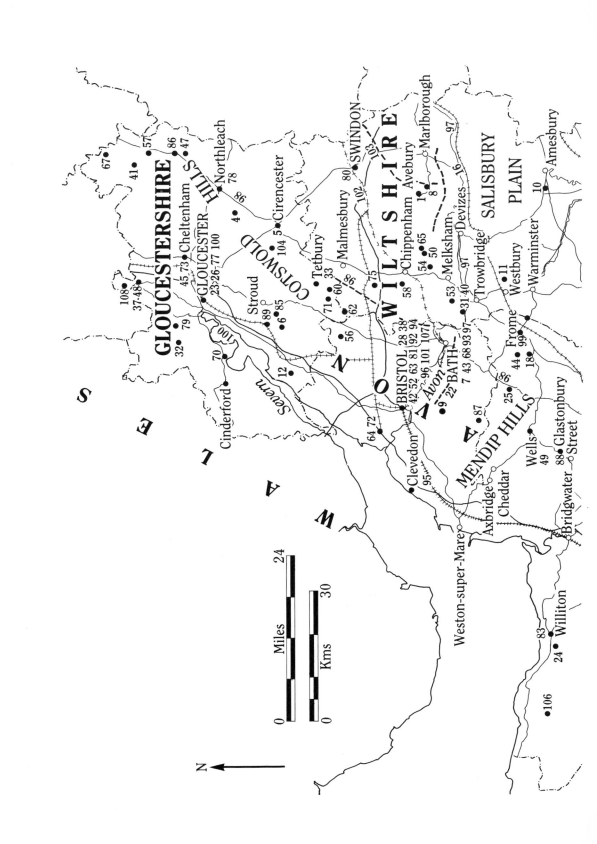

GLOUCESTERSHIRE

COTSWOLD

GLOUCESTER HILLS

WILTSHIRE

SALISBURY PLAIN

MENDIP HILLS

WALES

Severn

Avon

67
41
57
86
47
Northleach
78
Cheltenham
45 73
GLOUCESTER
23 26 77 100
86
4
Cirencester
104 5
Stroud
89
6 85
108
37-48
32 79
70
100
12
6
56
Tetbury
33
71 60
62 86
75
58
Malmesbury
102
80
SWINDON
103
Avebury
Marlborough
97
1
8
Devizes
16
Chippenham
54 65
50
Melksham
53
31 40 97
Trowbridge
11
Westbury
Warminster
Amesbury
10
28 38
BRISTOL 63 81 92 94
42 52 96 101 107
9 27 BATH
7 43 68 93 97
44
18
99
Frome
186
87
25
Clevedon
64 72
95
Weston-super-Mare
Axbridge
Cheddar
Wells
49
88 Glastonbury
Street
Bridgwater
83
24 Williton
106

Cinderford

N
O
V
A

E
S

W

Miles
0   24

Kms
0   30

N ←

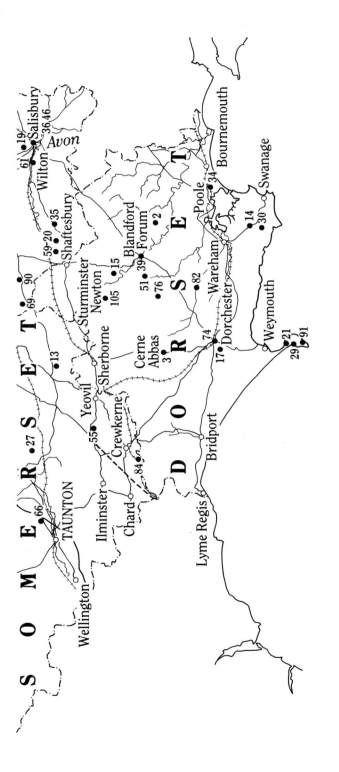

SOMERSET

Salisbury
36.46
19
61 Wilton
Avon

35 Shaftesbury
59-20

90
69

Sturminster Newton
Blandford Forum
15
39 105
51 76

2

BournemoutH

DORSET

Poole
34
Swanage
14
30
Wareham
82

13

Sherborne

Yeovil

27

Cerne Abbas
3

74
Dorchester
17

Weymouth
21
29 91

55

Crewkerne

84

TAUNTON
66

Ilminster

Chard

Bridport

Lyme Regis

Wellington

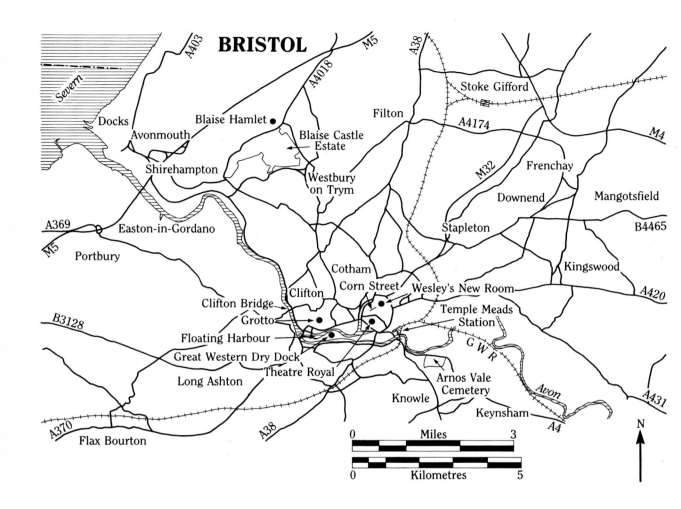

BRISTOL

Severn

Docks
Avonmouth
Shirehampton

A403

Blaise Hamlet •
Blaise Castle
Estate

A4018

M5

A38

Stoke Gifford

Filton

A4174

M4

A369
Easton-in-Gordano

M5
Portbury

Westbury
on Trym

M32

Frenchay
Downend

Mangotsfield

Stapleton

B4465

Kingswood

A420

B3128

Clifton Bridge
Grotto
Floating Harbour
Great Western Dry Dock
Theatre Royal

Long Ashton

Clifton

Cotham
Corn Street

Wesley's New Room

Temple Meads
Station

G W R

Arnos Vale
Cemetery

Knowle

Avon

A431

A370
Flax Bourton

A38

Keynsham
A4

N

| 0 | Miles | 3 |

| 0 | Kilometres | 5 |

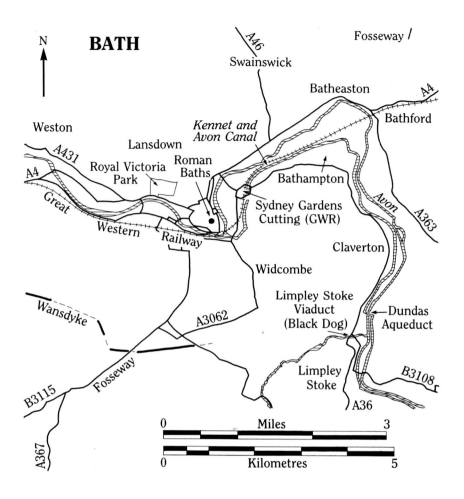

BATH

N

Weston

Lansdown

Kennet and Avon Canal

Swainswick

A46

Fosseway /

Batheaston

Bathford

A4

A431

A4

Royal Victoria Park

Great

Roman Baths

Western Railway

Bathampton

Sydney Gardens Cutting (GWR)

Avon

A363

Widcombe

Claverton

Wansdyke

A3062

Limpley Stoke Viaduct (Black Dog)

Dundas Aqueduct

B3115

Fosseway

Limpley Stoke

B3108

A367

A36

0	Miles	3

0	Kilometres	5